Angelo Mariani

Coca and its Therapeutic Application

Angelo Mariani

Coca and its Therapeutic Application

ISBN/EAN: 9783742831804

Manufactured in Europe, USA, Canada, Australia, Japa

Cover: Foto ©Gila Hanssen / pixelio.de

Manufactured and distributed by brebook publishing software (www.brebook.com)

Angelo Mariani

Coca and its Therapeutic Application

BRANCH OF COCA PLANT,
Showing Leaf, Flower and Seed.
(Specimen from hot-houses of M. Mariani, Neuilly, France.).

COCA

AND ITS

THERAPEUTIC APPLICATION

BY

ANGELO MARIANI

WITH ILLUSTRATIONS

THIRD EDITION.

NEW YORK
J. N. JAROS, 52 W. 15TH ST
1896.

The following pages are inscribed and respectfully dedicated to the medical profession, as a token of appreciation for the kind aid ever extended to me in my efforts to popularize that valuable addition to therapeutics, "Erythroxylon Coca."

ANGELO MARIANI.

41 Boulevard Haussmann,
   PARIS, FRANCE.

TO THE MEDICAL PROFESSION.

The physiological studies, researches, designs, etc., are made at our laboratory, Neuilly s/Seine, France, where, in connection with hot-houses, the study and cultivation of the Coca plant is carried on under my personal supervision, and am pleased to say have succeeded in producing large quantities of Coca plants, in all stages of growth and of various species, under all conditions of planting, by seeds, transplantation and grafting, all results being carefully watched and recorded.

I hereby extend the most cordial invitation to the medical profession and shall be happy to receive the visit of physicians who may be interested in the subject.

Respectfully,

ANGELO MARIANI.

41 Boulevard Haussmann,
PARIS, FRANCE.

OUTLINE OF COCA PLANT.
(Showing leaves and seeds. Nos. 1 and 2, Coca leaves seen by transmitted light.)

All illustrations in this volume have been specially prepared for this work, and are from original drawings from life by M. Mariani.

INTRODUCTION.

ACH race has its fashions and fancies. The Indian munches the betel; the Chinaman woos with passion the brutalizing intoxication of opium; the European occupies his idle hours or employs his leisure ones in smoking, chewing or snuffing tobacco. Guided by a happier instinct, the native of South America has adopted Coca. When young, he robs his father of it; later on, he devotes his first savings to its purchase. Without it he would fear vertigo on the summit of the Andes, and weaken at his severe labor in the mines. It is with him everywhere; even in his sleep he keeps his precious quid in his mouth.

But should Coca be regarded merely as a masticatory? And must we accept as irrevocable the decision of certain therapeutists: "Cocaine, worthless; Coca, superfluous drug"? (1)

For several years laryngologists such as: Fauvel, of France; Morell Mackenzie and Lennox Browne, of

(1) Nothnagel et Rossbach, *Nouveaux Éléments de Thérapeutique.*

England; and Elsberg, of America, had undertaken the defense of Coca.

Under such patronage Coca and its preparations were not slow in becoming popular.

Charles Fauvel was the first to make use of it as a general tonic, having a special action on the larynx; and to make known its anæsthetic and analgesic qualities.

Coca was further recommended, as it were empirically, against stomatitis, gingivitis, gastric disturbances, and phthisis (Rabuteau), *Eléments de thérapeutique et de pharmacologie*.

Although striking effects were obtained from this valuable medicine, its full worth was yet unknown and there was diversity of opinion as to its mode of action, until the communications of Köller, of Vienna, on Coca and Cocaine, appeared in 1884.

These interesting publications led to such general discussion among medical men, that nearly every one eagerly followed the work, and watched the splendid results obtained by the Viennese physician (now Professor of Ophthalmology in New York Polyclinic).

It is found that studies made of the active principles of Coca have entirely corroborated our previsions, and probably no subject has received greater attention than have the virtues of this little Peruvian shrub, formerly looked upon in Europe with so much indifference.

The scientific study of the principles of Coca may be considered as completed; and we believe that the time has arrived in which to summarize data regarding this therapeutic agent, so that the employment of our preparations may be based on positive clinical experience.

The aim of this modest work is to offer to the medical profession a short account of the history of Coca, and of the investigations which it has called forth up to the present day.

We propose to divide our subject into five parts.

1st. We will describe the botanical character of Coca, and also speak of its culture and the mode of gathering it.

2d. Its history, its properties and uses.

3d. The physiological researches made in the domain of Coca, devoting a special chapter to Cocaine.

4th. Its therapeutic application.

Finally we will quote some general conclusions and explanations regarding the method of using our different preparations, based on observations made by competent physicians in Europe and America.

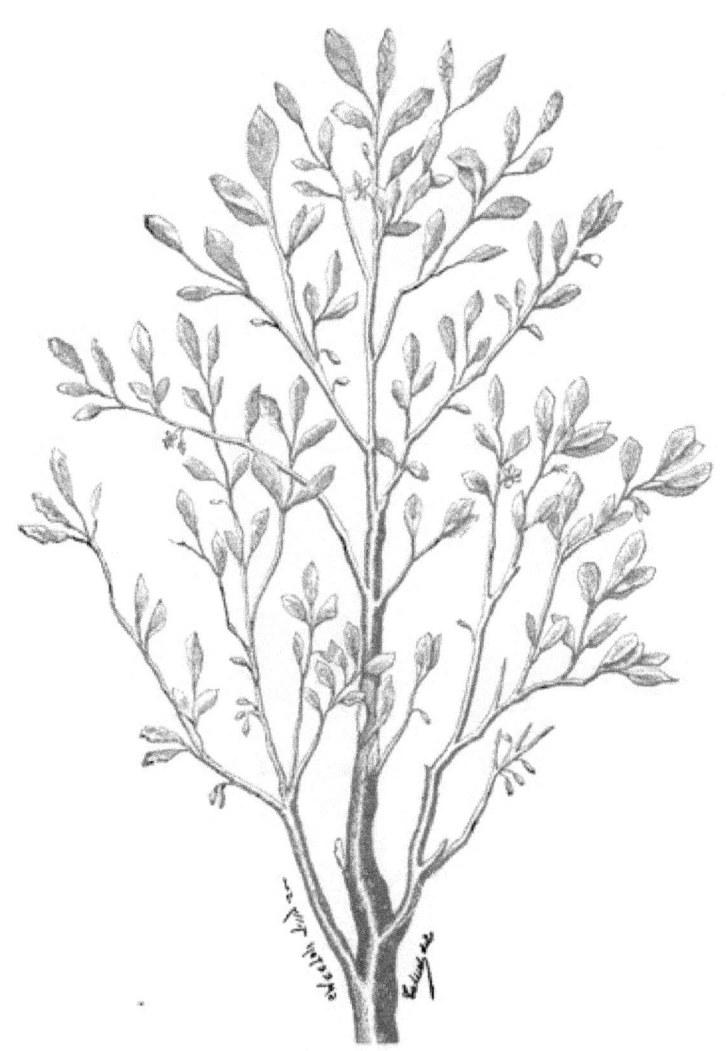

SPECIMEN OF THE COCA SHRUB.

(Grown in a Hot-house by Mr. Mariani showing general frail condition of the leaf.)

CHAPTER I.

ERYTHROXYLON COCA,

ITS BOTANICAL CHARACTER.

COCA is indigenous to South America. The different botanists disagree as to which exact family it should be assigned. Linnæus, De Candolle, Payer, Raymundi of Lima, Huntk, and others, place it in the family of the *Erythroxyleæ*, of which there exists but one genus, the *Erythroxylon*, while Jussien adopts another classification and places it in the family of the *Malpighiaceæ* (*genus Sethia*). Lamarck, on the contrary, believes that this plant should be classed among the family of Nerprem (Rhamneæ).

Erythroxylon Coca is a shrub which reaches a height of from six to nine feet and the stem is of about the thickness of a finger. In our climate it cannot thrive except in a hot-house, and there its height does not exceed one metre.

The root, rather thick, shows multiple and uniform divisions; its trunk is covered with a ridged bark, rugged, nearly always glabrous, and of a whitish color. Its boughs and branches, rather numerous, are alternant, sometimes covered with thorns when the plant is cultivated in a soil which is not well adapted to it.

The leaves, which fall spontaneously at the end of each season, are alternate, petiolate, with double intra-accillary stipules at the base. In shape they are elliptical-lanceolate, their size varying according to the nature of the plant or of the soil in which it grows.

The leaf of Coca gathered in Peru, of which we give two figures of the natural size, is generally larger and thicker than the leaf of the Bolivian Coca. It is also richer in the alkaloid, consequently much more bitter.

The Coca leaf from Bolivia, smaller than the Peruvian leaf, is as much esteemed as the latter, although it contains

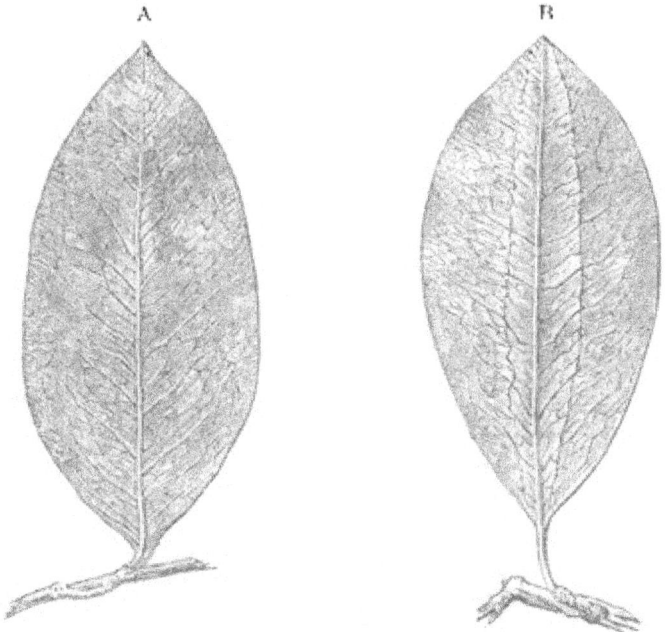

LEAVES OF PERUVIAN COCA, NATURAL SIZE.

A. Upper surface of the leaf.
B. Lower surface of the leaf, showing the longitudinal projections of the two sides of the midrib.

less of the alkaloid. It possesses so exquisite and so soft an aroma, indeed, that the *coqueros* seek it in preference to any other.

The Coca leaves of Brazil and Colombia are much smaller than those of Peru and Bolivia. Their color is much paler. Containing but traces of the alkaloid they are not bitter, and possess a pleasant, but very volatile aroma.

One of the most important characteristics of the Coca leaf is the disposition of its nervures; parallel with the midrib two longitudinal projections are to be seen, which, starting from the base of the leaf, extend in a gentle curve to its point.

LEAVES OF BOLIVIAN COCA, NATURAL SIZE.

(Lower surface.)

The upper surface of these leaves is of a beautiful green tint; the lower surface of a paler green, except, however, near the midrib. At this point, there is a strip of green

LEAF OF COCA OF COLOMBIA, NATURAL SIZE.

darker than the rest, which becomes brown in the withered leaves.

The flowers, small, regular and hermaphrodite, white or greenish yellow, are found either alone or in groups in little bunches of cyme at the axil of the leaves or bracts, which take their place on certain branches. The disposition into cymes is that most commonly met with. They are supported by a slender pedicel, somewhat inflated at the top, the length of which does not exceed one centi-

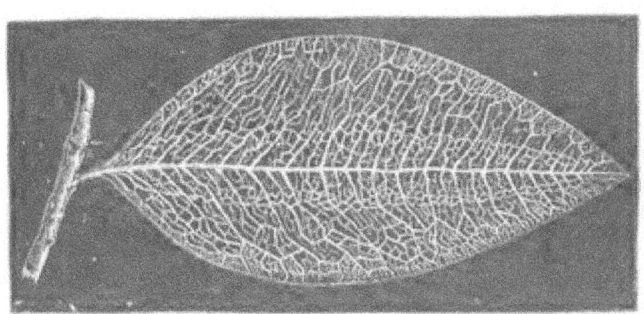

NERVURES OF THE LEAF OF PERUVIAN COCA, SEEN BY TRANSMITTED LIGHT. NATURAL SIZE.

metre. The sepals, joined at the base and lanceolated, are of a green tint with a whitish top. The petals, half a centimetre in length, pointed, concave inside and yellowish white, exhale a rather pleasant odor. They are provided with an exterior appendage, of the same color and of the same con-

Seeds of Coca.

sistency, surmounted on each side with an ascending fimbriated leaf, irregularly triangular in shape. The stamens, at first joined in a tube for one-third of their length, afterward separate into white subulated strings, provided with an obtuse ovoid anther which extends a little beyond the petals. The ovary is ovoid in shape and green in color, thickening at the top into a yellowish glandular tissue. The style which rises above it separates into three diverging branches, provided with orbicular papilliform bodies at their extremity, obliquely inserted into the slender patina.

The fruit is a drupe of an elongated ovoid form, being a little more than a centimetre in length, of a reddish color when fresh, and having a tender, thickish pulp inclosing a seed. This seed shows longitudinal furrows and alternate vertical projections which make its division irregularly hexagonal. When the fruit is dried, the skin assumes a brownish color, shrivels up and molds itself on the protuberances and irregularities of the seed.

CULTIVATION OF COCA.

Erythroxylon Coca appears to have come originally from Peru, and from there its cultivation was carried into Bolivia, Ecuador, New Grenada, and Brazil, in a word, throughout the entire torrid zone of South America.

For some time, as a result of the extended consumption of Coca and for a still stronger reason, now that the day is at hand when the consumption of Coca will assume greater proportions, numerous plantations of Coca trees have been laid out in regions where that shrub was formerly unknown. We take pleasure in recording that these attempts have proved successful in the Antilles, thanks to the disinterested sacrifices of our friend, Dr. Bétancès. It is also with pleasure that we present anew an interesting communication made by the learned doctor to the "Société d'Acclimatation de France" as appeared in the *Revue Diplomatique*, 17th of March, 1888.

"Dr. Bétancès has succeeded in acclimatizing Coca in the Antilles. At considerable expense and after numerous shipments of seeds and the transportation of plants (this with the greatest difficulty) to Porto Rico and San Domingo, Dr. Bétancès had the pleasure of receiving a fine branch of Coca in full bloom, which was sent to him by Monseigneur Mereño, Archbishop of San Domingo. This twig,

BRANCH OF COCA. NATURAL SIZE.

Sent by Monseigneur de Mereño, Archbishop of San Domingo, to Dr. Bétancès, Paris.

which the members of the Society were enabled to examine, excited the most lively curiosity and won the commendation of M. Geoffroy Saint-Hilaire. It was raised from a plant which had been only eighteen months under cultivation."

"In Porto Rico the plant reaches a greater height than in Peru.

"A box filled with beautiful leaves has also been received by Dr. Bétancès and forwarded to Mr. Mariani. This also came from Monseigneur Mereño.

"It is therefore evident that the plant can be cultivated in the Antilles and that it may become a source of wealth to that country."

Plantations like this would probably thrive in Corsica or Algeria, countries where the temperature at certain points is somewhat analogous to that of the tropics.

It is a fact that this shrub does not attain its complete development except in countries where the mean temperature is from fifteen to eighteen degrees centigrade.

But heat does not suffice; great humidity is also necessary to Coca Therefore it is met with principally on the sides of hills and at the bottom of wooded valleys which abound on both sides of the Cordillieras. Unfortunately, these regions are rather distant from the coast and they are, furthermore, devoid of easy means of communication; it is above all to this particular cause, the difficulty of transportation, that we must attribute the relatively high price of Coca leaves.

The cultivation of Coca trees is begun by sowing the seed in beds called *Almazigos*. As soon as the plant appears it is protected from the heat of the sun by means of screens and matting; when it reaches a height of from 40 to 50 centimetres, it is transferred to furrows 18 centimetres in length by 7 in depth, care being taken that each plant is separated from its neighbor by a distance of a foot.

During the first year maize is sown in the interspaces, rapidly overreaching the shrub, and taking the place of the screens and mats.

The growth of the shrub is rather rapid, reaching its full height in about five years. But the time when it becomes productive precedes that at which it attains its complete height by about 3½ years after being planted. After that, when the season has been especially damp, it yields as often as four times a year.

Attempts have been made to acclimatize it in Europe, but so far without success. As early as 1869 the cultivation of it was tried in the Botanical Garden of Hyères, but no satisfactory result was obtained. We presented, in 1872, two samples to the appreciative and learned director of the Garden of Acclimatization of Paris, M. Geoffroy Saint-Hilaire, and notwithstanding all the care taken of the young plants, they failed to reach their full growth. Several frail Coca plants may be seen in the conservatories of the *Jardin des Plantes de Paris*, in the Botanical Gardens of London, of Brussels, etc., likewise at several great horticulturists' of Gand, notably Van Houten's. As may be seen by the large colored engraving (1) and by the branch engraved above, these specimens of *Erythroxylon Coca* are very far from giving an idea of the plant growing in the open air, in a soil and

BRANCH OF COCA,
as grown in a hot-house.

(1) This cut represents the Coca shrub presented by Mr. A. Mariani to the Paris Botanical Gardens.

under a temperature that are favorable to its development, as shown by the leaves of Peruvian Coca, illustrated above, and which come from one of the newest *haciendas* of Santa-Anna, belonging to M. M.-P. Concha, bordering on the territory of a savage tribe of Antis or Campas, on the Urubanba river, which joins the Amazon in latitude 12° S., longitude 75° W.

GATHERING OF COCA.

The plant begins to yield when it is about a year and a half old.

The leaf is the only part of the plant used.

It should be gathered in dry weather; this is entrusted generally to women, and simply consists in plucking each leaf with the fingers.

The leaves are received into aprons, carefully carried under sheds, to shelter them from the rain and dampness, dried, and then packed.

We quote from the *Voyage dans la région du Titicaca*, by Paul Marcoy, the following passage ("Tour of the World," May, 1877): "Of all the valleys of the Carabaya group, Ituata is the one where Coca is cultivated on the largest scale. They were then at the height of the work, peons and peonnes were following each other through the plantations of the shrub, so dear to the natives that a decree of 1825 placed it in the crown of the arms of Peru, alongside of the vicunia and cornucopia, or horn-of-plenty. Men and women carried a cloth slung across the shoulders in which were placed the leaves, as they gathered them one by one. These leaves, spread out on large awnings, were exposed to the sun for two or three days, then packed up in bags of about one metre in size, and sent off to all parts of the territory.

"This gathering of the Coca is just such an occasion for rejoicing for the natives of the valleys, as reaping-time and harvests are for our peasants. On the day when the gathering of the leaves is finished both sexes that have taken part in the work assemble and celebrate, in dances and libations, the pleasure they experience in having finished their labors."

In 1851, the annual production of Bolivia was estimated to be more than 400,000 certos (600,000 kilogrammes) of Coca leaves, of which three-quarters came from the province of Yungas.

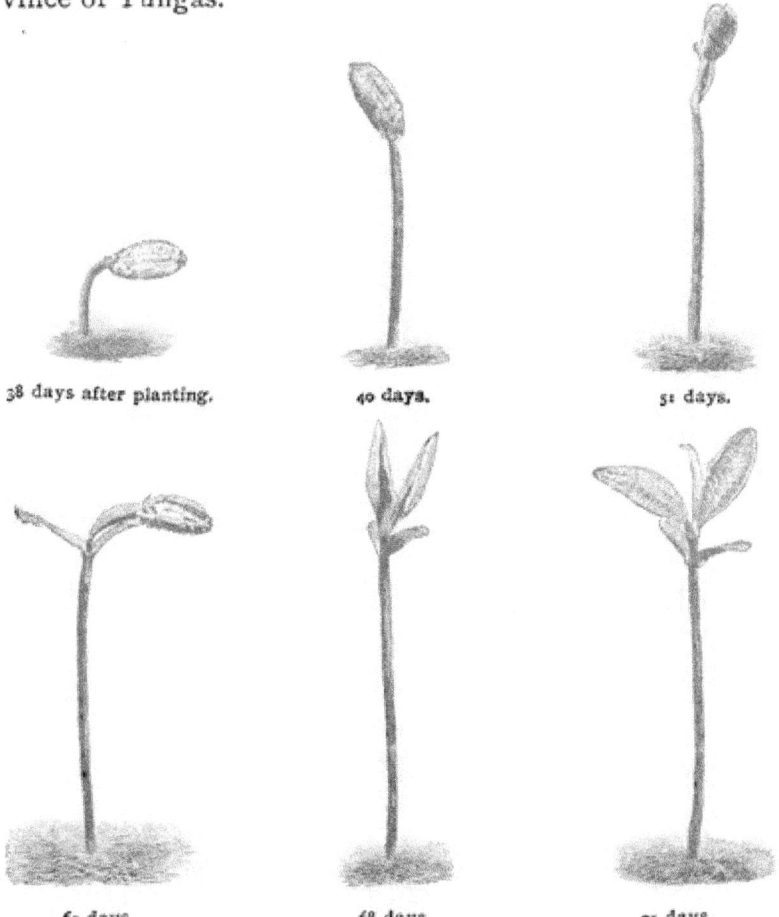

Observation of Growing Seeds in Hot-houses of M. Mariani.

ERYTHROXYLON COCA.

(Specimen of a branch grown in hot-houses of Mr. Mariani.)

COCA PLANT

Obtained by transplanting; eight months.

(Hot-houses of Mariani.)

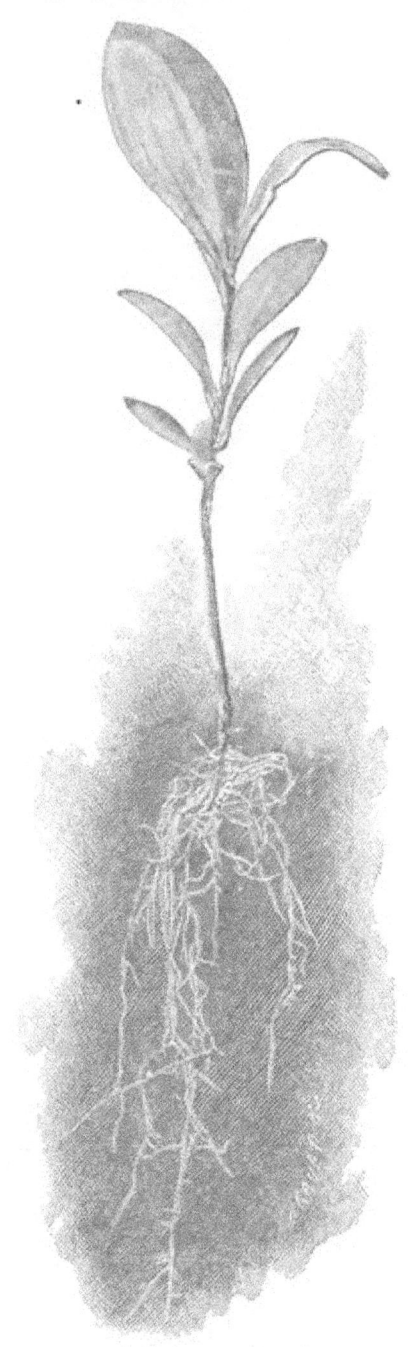

COCA PLANT
Obtained from seed; eight months.
(Hot-houses of Mariani.)

CHAPTER II.

HISTORY OF COCA.

COCA has been known from time immemorial in South America. At the time when Pizarro landed on the Peruvian coast, the leaf of Coca was held in great esteem among the natives; it was considered to be a divine plant, a living representation of the Deity, a fetish of wonderful and supernatural qualities, and the fields where it grew were reverenced as sanctuaries. Not everybody was allowed to make use of it; its use was the privilege of the nobles and of the priests, and among the greatest rewards that the sovereign could give his subjects, the privilege of chewing Coca leaves was most highly esteemed.

However strange such a superstition may appear, it is indisputable, and all authors that have published the account of the conquest of the Indies corroborate it. It will suffice for us to quote the testimony of Joseph Acosta, who says in every letter, of his natural and moral history of the Indies, of the East as well as of the West, published in 1653:

"The Indians esteem it highly, and during the reign of the Incas, the common people were not allowed to use Coca without the permission of the Governor."

The disappearance of the empire of the Incas, far from diminishing the importance of Coca, on the contrary gave a very much greater scope to its popularity. The natives profited by their freedom from the restrictions imposed by the native rulers in regard to the consumption of Coca, and soon the use of this leaf became so common that it has been compared by every one interested in the question to the use of tobacco by us; and, as it has justly been added, without its objections. There is no more likelihood of seeing a smoker embark without his tobacco than an Indian begin work or undertake a journey unless his *chuspa* (pouch) is full of Coca leaves. Three or four times

NATIVES OF COLOMBIA CHEWING COCA.

a day he sits down, takes some leaves, puts them one by one into his mouth and rolls them into an *aculio* (quid), adding a little *llipta* (lime), which he takes from his ever-present *poporo*. The *poporo* is a little gourd, bored at the mouth on the upper part, in which the Indian keeps his *llipta*. This *llipta* is a white powder composed of ashes of vegetables and of calcined shells pulverized, with which the consumers of Coca have been accustomed, from the most remote times, to season their quid. It is, really, an alkaline substance intended to isolate the different principles of the leaf and to make the action of the Coca more prompt.

Among those inhabitants of South America, with whom the use of Coca did not extend to the lower classes until after the reign of the Incas, and who reserved for themselves, as we have seen, the right of chewing the Coca leaves, the consumption of Coca by children is strictly prohibited. They do not indulge in this luxury except in secret, and it appears to them all the sweeter because it is forbidden. But nearly always their breath, charged with the tell-tale odor of Coca, betrays them on approaching their parents, and the latter make them pay for the pleasure which they have stolen, and to which they are not entitled until they are of age, with very severe punishment. Only when they have grown up will they be allowed to chew Coca and to carry the *poporo*, which they do not relinquish even in the grave.

On coming of age the young Indian is consigned to an old woman, who keeps him a few hours in her hut to initiate him in the mysteries of man's estate.

After this ceremony she gives him the *chuspa* (Coca pouch), invests him with the *poporo* and consecrates him a *coquero*. One should see with what pride the young Indian leaves the threshold of the sacred cabin, which he entered as a child scarcely a few hours before and from which he departs a man, that is to say, carrying the *chuspa* and the *poporo*, and able to chew with impunity, before the old people, this precious leaf which had been forbidden him until then.

No happiness is comparable to his! See with what an important air he draws forth the Coca leaves from his *chuspa*, as he rolls them in his fingers to make a large quid of them, which he carries to his mouth, moistens delightingly with saliva, and places under his jaws and against his cheeks. He is seen holding carefully in his right hand the little stick, the extremity of which he is going to moisten by putting it into his mouth, and which he will dip into the *poporo* in order that the *llipta* may adhere to its moistened part.

He carefully carries the part of his little stick covered with *llipta* to his quid, and thus performs the operation of mixing the alkaline powder with the masticated leaf, It is at this moment that the quid of Coca affords the young adult the most delightful sensation. His jaws munch it slowly, his tongue collects and rolls it up against the left cheek, all the *papillæ* of his mouth refresh themselves deliciously with the soothing and aromatic juices of the precious leaf, and by the slow and measured motions of deglutition, he carries with delight the precious juice into the pharynx and thence to the stomach. While he is accomplishing this important operation, his eyes swim with beatitude, over his entire countenance is diffused an expression of content and unutterable joy, and his right hand slowly turns the little stick around the upper part of the *poporo*, where are deposited little by little the particles of *llipta* and masticated Coca, which on leaving his mouth adhere to its extremity.

The only occupation of the first days of the adult is the much-loved quid of Coca and the encrusting of his gourd, which we cannot do better than compare to the coating of the pipe, with this difference that our confirmed smokers blacken hundreds of their pipes during their existence, while the Indian encrusts only one gourd in his whole life; so that by the thickness of the crust formed around a *poporo*, it is possible to judge the age of its owner. This crust, which hardly ever exceeds the thickness of a ring on the *poporo* of a young Indian, ends by reaching the dimension of the pileus of a large mushroom on the *poporo* of an old man.

The crust is produced by the particles of Coca and *llipta* mixed with saliva which are deposited little by little about the mouth of the *poporo* by smearing with the stick.

These deposits are brought about in an almost imperceptible manner. It is only after some months that the surface of the *poporo*, on which the chewer continually turns the little stick, becomes covered with a hardly perceptible layer of calcareous substance; at the end of two or three years the superimposed layers form a ring which grows larger from year to year, and which finally attains the thickness we have spoken of above.

Small stick for extracting the Llipta from the poporo.

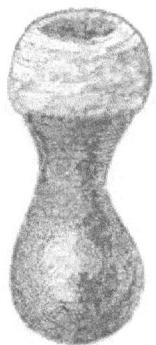 

1. Poporo of a youth.   2. Poporo of a man in his prime.   3. Poporo of an old man.

As we have said before, the Indian never parts with his *poporo*, let him be awake or asleep, at home or on his travels, the *poporo* is always attached to his belt. An Indian would part with all he holds most dear in the world, all, except his *poporo*.

We have the rare and good fortune to possess a *poporo*, of which we give a picture (fig. 3). It is, we believe, the only specimen existing in Europe. We owe it to the kindness of M. Gauguet, who has made numerous voyages to Colombia, where he has been able to establish so much sympathy among the natives that one of their old chiefs, who was specially indebted, did not fear to depart from all custom and to incur the contempt of his companions, by offering him, as a pledge of friendship, the object to which he attached the greatest value—his *poporo!* (1)

Thus the great importance that an Indian attaches to Coca is easily shown. It should be recognized, moreover, that the first conquerors of the country did not fail to countenance the passion of the vanquished for the national plant. In fact, they quickly recognized that the habit of consuming Coca might become an excellent source of revenue; and Garcillasco de la Véga, a half-breed of the first generation, tells us that in his time a part of the impost was paid to the conqueror in the form of Coca leaves. The benefits which were derived from the traffic in this plant were such that at a certain time the revenues of the bishop and of the canons of the cathedral of Cuzco came from the tithe on these leaves.

There was, moreover, another object in favoring the use of Coca among the Indians. The latter were treated, as is known, as if they were beasts of burden, and their oppressors were not slow to recognize the fact that they furnished much better labor when they consumed Coca.

We shall see, further on, that the recognition of this fact, the correctness of which cannot be disputed, and which served to excite the rapacity of the conquering savages of that time, has become to-day the means of furnishing one of the most valuable aids to contemporary therapeutics.

The particular favor in which the plant was held in the beginning of the conquest, was destined to suffer some disturbance. In the seventeenth century, for example, the religious quibbles regaining the ascendancy in public affairs, some sedate theologians pretended that Coca was an aliment, and that under this name the use of it should be prohibited to young people and before the communion. The question was vigorously contested, and

(1) Mr. Mariani has presented to the Academy of Medicine a plaster cast of this very *poporo*, in his possession.

there is no doubt that the consumption of Coca would have sustained a very decided blow had not Prince don Alonzo de la Pina Montenegro declared that the plant contained no alimentary principle. This point we shall presently consider from a scientific point of view.

Although the inhabitants of the Indies attach so much importance to the use of Coca, this product can not be acclimatized in our hemisphere, and our fathers who took up the use of tobacco with so much eagerness remained indifferent to Coca. Perhaps this indifference should be attributed to the exaggerations of the first importers, who coming to Europe still imbued with the legends gathered in the New World ascribed supernatural qualities to the new plant. The exaggeration of these statements soon became apparent. From this it was only a step to a denial even of its existence. And thus, for more than two centuries, we were deprived of the advantages to be derived from the judicious use of the plant

It should not be believed, however, that the various writers during these two centuries remained entirely silent regarding Coca. The study of the properties of the plant was still a field of research for a number of learned men, small, it is true, but they well knew that side by side with fiction, which they rejected, there was a reality that it were better to accept.

We further observe, that Claude Duret, a magistrate of Moulins, who wrote a book, printed in 1605, on *The Marvellous and Wonderful Plants in Nature*, mentions Coca as one of the most worthy to figure in his colleccion.

Nicholas Monardes in the *General History of Plants*, published in Lyons in 1653, calls attention likewise to the properties of Coca.

In the seventeenth century, l'abbé Longuerue, who was a theologian, an historian, and a philologist, speaking of the Spanish colonies in South America, says, in regard to the mines explored in Peru: "The negroes can not work in the mines, they all die. Hardly any but the natives are able to endure this labor, and then it is necessary to relieve them frequently and that they should chew Coca, without which the quicksilver vapors would kill them."

Linnæus says that Coca possesses: "the penetrating aroma of vegetable stimulants, the astricting and fortifying virtues of an astringent, the antispasmodic qualities of bitters, and the mucilaginous nutritive propertics of analeptics or of alimentary plants. This leaf," he continues, "exhibits with energy its action on all parts of the animal economy: *Olido in nervos, sapido in fibras utroque in fluido.*"

Father don Antonio Julian wrote: "This plant is a preventive against many diseases, a restorative of lost strength, and is capable of prolonging human life. It is sincerely to be regretted that so many poor families do not possess this preventive of hunger and thirst; that so many employees and laborers should be deprived of this means of maintaining their strength in the midst of continuous toil; that so many old and young men engaged in the arduous task of study and the accomplishment of their undertakings are unable to derive the beneficial results of this plant to guard against the exhaustion of the vital spirits, debility of the brain, and weakness of the stomach, which are frequent results of continuous study."

Böerhaave (*Inst. phys.* § 68), states that: "the saliva charged with all the bitter and mucilaginous principles of Coca carries to the stomach, in addition to vital strength, a veritable nutritive which, digested and converted into an abundant and nutritious chyle, enters into the circulation and is converted into the material necessary to sustain the human economy."

We shall not stop to quote the different writings of observers who have interested themselves in Coca. It may be inferred from the preceding statements that Coca possesses this particular character, viz., of enabling those who make use of it to withstand the greatest fatigue. Men employed in hard work in mines, couriers obliged to traverse mountainous countries difficult of travel without being able to take much rest, in a word, persons subject to overwork in every way, all agree in recognizing the strengthening and nerve-fortifying action of Coca. It supports them, economizes their forces, prevents their succumbing to lassitude—in short, augments their vitality.

When the Indian has a good supply of Coca he undertakes, without the slightest fear, the most difficult and longest voyages, even into fever-stricken countries.

When he passes before an *apacheeta* (a quadrangular mound which the natives raise on the sides of the roads at certain points for a halting-place), the Indian divests himself of his wraps, takes his quid of Coca from his mouth, always after having previously exhausted it, and, in order to draw down upon it the blessing of Pachacamac, their sovereign master of the world, he throws it against the consecrated hillock. Thus, that which particularly characterizes these kinds of *tumuli* are the green splashes of Coca with which they are literally covered.

The name of *coqueros* is given to the chewers of Coca. It seems that this plant procured for them dreams like those to which hachisch gives rise.

In native therapeutics, this plant is used to dress ulcers and all kinds of sores. The Indians also use it to combat asthma, jaundice, colic, etc.

Coca is consumed chiefly in Peru, Bolivia, Colombia, and Brazil. Since 1863—the time from which our first efforts to popularize it date—its use has rapidly become general, and it may be stated that to-day it is known and used in all civilized countries.

CHAPTER III.

PHYSIOLOGY OF COCA.

IT is to empiricism and that alone that we owe our first knowledge of the physiological action of Coca. There is nothing surprising in that, for empiricism is nothing more, in reality, than unconscious observation.

The Indians, who from time immemorial consumed so great a quantity of Coca leaves, did not do so merely from religious sentiment which deified the leaves of Coca, they well knew that they would derive great benefit from its use; they knew it only too well, since it is to that cause that we must attribute the legendary accounts given by the first authors who wrote on Coca.

This veneration for Coca arose, as we have seen, from its wonderful qualities. There are indeed, in this direction, some truly extraordinary accounts which should not be dismissed without notice, as they are given in good faith.

Unanué, of Lima, relates that at the siege of La Paz, Bolivia, in 1781, only those inhabitants who had taken Coca were able to endure hunger and fatigue. Nearly all of the soldiers perished, deprived, as they were of food and overcome by forced marches, except those who had taken the precaution to provide themselves with Coca leaves.

It must not be believed that this prolonged fast, sustained by the use of Coca, wastes the strength and is injurious to the appetite. Indeed, according to the statemen', of all authors, the Indians who pass an entire day without eating, notwithstanding the hardship of forced marches, content themselves with chewing Coca leaves, and eat very heartily in the evening.

"The Indians who accompanied me on my voyage," says Weddel, "chewed Coca leaves all day, neither drinking, eating, nor showing any signs of fatigue But at evening they replenished their stomachs like men who were completely famished, and I can assure you that I have sometimes seen them devour at one meal more aliment than I could have consumed in two days." We will see, further on, that it is in exciting the cerebro-medullary and nervous muscular functions, in part, and partly in producing a soothing effect on the mucous membrane of the stomach, that Coca produces these wonderful results in the conservation of energy without the tortures of hunger, notwithstanding the deprivation of aliment.

After this abstract of the well-known and recognized properties of Coca leaves, we will proceed to the medical study undertaken regarding this subject.

In 1859 Niemann discovered the active principle of the leaves of Coca, to which he gave the name of Cocaine, though, in fact, the discovery of this alkaloid should be attributed to Gardeke, who had separated it in 1855 under the name of *Erythroxyline*.

The work of Demarle appeared in that same year, on "The Coca of Peru" (1), in which he pointed out certain properties attributed by him to the alkaloid that the leaves of the plant contained, and which he studied. He remarked, among other things, the dilatation of the pupils, which he had noticed in his own case after having taken a dose of Coca; the absence of taste for a greater or less length of time after crushing some leaves with his teeth and letting them remain in the mouth.

(1) Dr. Demarle, *Essay on Peruvian Coca*, *Thèse de Paris*, 1862.

Mantegazza has studied the effect of Coca and, according to this author, it acts as a stimulant on the nervous system, the respiration, and the circulation.

A dose of fifteen to twenty grammes of Coca produces an increase of the heart-beat, increasing pulse, and finally a rise in temperature. Mantegazza observed on himself that, under the influence of such a dose, his pulse increased from 65 to 124. Moreno, who repeated the same experiment, obtained similar results. The temperature and respiration are increased in the same proportion as the circulation.

The same dose, or even a weaker one, produces a remarkably stimulating effect on the nervous system. It is from this stimulating effect that Coca makes one more active and vigorous and enables those to accomplish more work who, without it, would soon be overcome with more or less fatigue. The use of larger doses (60 grammes for example) has caused intoxication, accompanied by sensation of happiness, which makes everything appear under a favorable aspect. Mantegazza, who experienced this intoxication, describes his sensations in an animated style, which recalls that of the Oriental legends: " Borne on the wings of two Coca leaves, I flew about in the spaces of 77,438 worlds, one more splendid than another. I prefer a life of ten years with Coca to one of a hundred thousand without it. It seemed to me that I was separated from the whole world, and I beheld the strangest images, most beautiful in color and in form that can be imagined."

In 1868, Moreno y Maïz made some researches into the physiological action of Cocaine, and explained them in an interesting thesis which he read before the Faculty of Paris (1).

At about the same time, Lippmann, of Strasbourg, devoted his labors to the same subject, but his investigations

(1) Moreno y Maïz, *Thèse de Paris*, 1868:

did not yield the same results. He says that he could not establish the anæsthetic properties of the plant. (1)

After Moreno y Maïz, Dr. Gazeau (2), in 1870, studied the stimulating effect of Coca on nutrition, and found that it increased the pulse and respiration, assisted digestion, increased urinary excretion, and strengthened the nervous system. This author arrived at the conclusion that Coca prolongs life and promotes muscular energy. He advises its use, locally, for stomatitis, gingivitis, aphthous ulceration, and generally for painful and difficult digestion, gastric disturbance in phthisis, and also for obesity.

It was Charles Fauvel who first described the anæsthetizing effect of Coca on the pharyngeal mucous membrane (3). Thanks to this circumstance, he has been able to derive much benefit from the use of Coca in granular pharyngitis which is generally unaffected by any other kind of treatment.

Fauvel further showed that the stimulating effect which Coca exercises on all the muscles of the economy, appears to manifest itself specially on all the muscles of the larynx. Hence his apt qualification of the drug, "a tensor *par excellence* of the vocal cords."

In 1880, Von Arep published the results of his physiological researches with Cocaine. He spoke of its double effect on the nervous extremities and on the central nervous system.

We approach, on leaving this epoch, the really scientific era, that is to say, that of physiological experiments.

All the experiments having been made with Cocaine, we shall speak of it in the next chapter, which will be devoted exclusively to the study of this alkaloid.

Before closing, we will mention that it has been claimed frequently that Coca was aphrodisiac. The fact that the

(1) Lippmann, *Thèse de Strasbourg*, 1868.
(2) Gazeau, *Thèse de Paris*, 1870.
(3) *Gazette des Hôpitaux*, Paris, March 12, 1877.

Peruvian Venus was represented as holding in her hand a leaf of Coca, was suggested as a proof in support of this opinion. Dr. Unanué speaks of "certain coqueros, eighty years of age and over, and yet capable of such prowess as young men in the prime of life would be proud of."

Let us here add that the so-called unhappy consequences of the abuse of Coca are really much more rare than those produced even by tobacco, alcohol or opium.

The constant use of reasonable doses of Coca appears to produce a diametrically opposite effect, and the authors, who have had occasion to see a great number of Coca consumers, report cases of astonishing longevity among the Indian coqueros (Tschudy, Campbell, Mantegazza, Unanué). They add that these instances are far from being exceptional.

COCAINE.

I.—A CHEMICAL STUDY. (1)

Cocaine is a crystallized alkaloid which Niemann, a pupil of Prof. Wœhler, succeeded in extracting, in 1859, from some leaves of *Erythroxylon Coca* and to which he gave the following formula:

$$C^{32} H^2 O Az O^2.$$

Before it was known to him, Wackenroder, Johnston, Gardeke and Maclagan analyzed this plant without succeeding in the isolation of its active principle.

Some important works undertaken on this subject by Lassen, Humann and R. Pérey are also quoted.

(1) Rigolet. *Thèse de Paris*, 1885.

Properties.—Cocaine is colorless, odorless, and bitter to the taste. It crystallizes in the shape of oblique rhomboid prisms of from four to six facets.

It is very soluble in water, less soluble in alcohol, and absolutely insoluble in ether. It does not vaporize below 98°, but if the temperature is greatly increased it is decomposed. It possesses a strongly alkaline reaction.

United with acids it forms salts which are very difficult to crystallize.

Those which have been obtained from it are: the salicylate, oxalate, hydrobromide, sulphate, acetate, and finally the hydrochlorate, which forms an exception to the general rule, and is obtained more easily in the crystalline form than any other.

The solutions of the salts of Cocaine are precipitated by the caustic alkalies, carbonate of sodium, carbonate of ammonium, the alkaline bicarbonates, the bichloride of mercury, the protochloride of tin, bichloride of platinum, and by ammonia, which, added in excess, redissolves the precipitate formed by it. Iodine water, iodized potassium iodide, and picric acid precipitate the solutions of salts of Cocaine. When Cocaine is heated to 100° in a sealed tube with concentrated hydrochloric acid, it separates into benzoic acid and a new base, for which M. Wœhler has proposed the name of *Ecgonine*. Lassen has discovered another nitrogenous base resulting from the separation of Cocaine—*hygrine*.

Preparation.—The process used by Niemann for obtaining Cocaine is as follows:

This chemist digested Coca leaves, cut into very small pieces, in alcohol (at 55°), for several days, adding sulphuric acid. The tincture which resulted from this operation was separated by expression, filtered, and treated with slaked lime. The liquid, which was primarily of a greenish-brown, was both divested of a part of its chlorophyll and also of a certain waxy substance. Niemann then neutralized this with sulphuric acid and evaporated it over a water-bath. The residue was then treated with water, which caused the separation of the rest of the chlorophyll and of the sulphate of Cocaine that it contained, and which was precipitated by means of the carbonate of sodium. He separated it finally with ether and purified it by several re-crystallizations in alcohol. This process was modified by Lassen, who precipitated the aqueous solution with the subacetate of lead.

In this way he was able to obtain about six grammes of Cocaine from a kilogramme of Coca leaves.

Moreno y Maïz proposed a third process. He mixed intimately, slaked lime with finely-pulverized Coca leaves, letting the mixture stand for nearly twenty-four hours, in order that the lime might react suitably on the alkaloid, imitating in that, the Indian who mixes with his quid the *llipta*, of which we have already spoken. He afterward lixiviates it with alcohol at 40°.

II.—PHYSICAL STUDY.

We have reviewed the works of the different authors who occupied themselves with Coca; their various labors, although very interesting, did not reach the famous discovery of local anæsthesia, and it is to Köller, of Vienna (1), that the honor belongs of having brought to light the remarkable effect of Cocaine when applied to the conjunctival membrane.

This soon awakened general curiosity. From all quarters came works on the subject. Reuss, Kœnigstein, Jellinck, Schrotter, Knapp and others hastened to give to the profession the result of their researches.

In France enthusiasm was not less strong, nor less

(1) Soc. imp. royale des médecins de Vienne, Oct. 17, 1884.

prompt, all those whom this discovery interested undertook a series of experiments with Cocaine (1).

Among the first experimenters we must mention specially, Prof. Panas, Prof. Vulpian, Prof. Dujardin-Beaumetz, Dr. Terrier, Dr. Trousseau, Dr. Dehenne.

Prof. Panas reports in a communication made by him to the Académie de Médecine (2) what he has observed.

He states, besides, that in nearly all respects his personal investigations are confirmatory of those made by Köller.

About five minutes after a few drops of a solution of hydrochloride of Cocaine composed of 0.5 gramme of that salt to a gramme of distilled water have been instilled into the eye, anæsthesia of the conjunctival mucous membrane of the cornea begins to manifest itself and reaches the deep parts in about fifteen or twenty minutes if the instillations are repeated every five minutes.

At the same time there is a certain amount of mydriasis, but this is less pronounced than that produced by atropine. This pupillary dilatation, which is more perceptible in young subjects and not in glaucomatous states, lasts, at least, for twenty-four hours. With that occurs a slight paralysis of the ciliary muscle.

"On account of this," says Professor Panas, "Cocaine should be placed among the slightly mydriatic substances of which the passing effect might be utilized for ophthalmoscopic explorations of the fundus of the eye, under the same head as, and better than, homatropine."

According to M. Dujardin-Beaumetz, Cocaine not only deadens sensibility, but it can further be utilized with morphinomaniacs as a substitute for morphine without presenting the objections of the latter substance; and he adds that subcutaneous injections made with this alkaloid are not irritating (*Bulletin de l'Académie de Médecine*, session of the 18th of November, 1884).

(1) Rigolet, *Thèse de Paris*, 1888.
(2) M. Panas. Communication à l'Acad. de Médecine, November, 1884.

Prof. Vulpian, at the outset, communicated to the Académie des Sciences the results of his interesting physiological researches with the chlorhydrate of Cocaine.

M. Vulpian, after observing similar anæsthetic and analgesic effects on the eye in animals as already shown in man, resulting from an instillation between the eyelids of a few drops of solution of hydrochlorate of Cocaine, and also perceiving under these conditions the mydriatic action of the salt, noticed a protrusion of the ocular globe when he injected 0.10 centigramme of hydrochloride of Cocaine of a one to one hundred aqueous solution into the saphenous vein of a non-curarized dog, and that it occurred almost immediately after throwing the liquid into the vessel. Instantly the eyelids were seen to separate and the pupillary orifice to enlarge. "This," says he, "is an effect which exactly recalls the results of faradization of the upper extremity of the cervical sympathetic nerve cut transversely."

Complete anæsthesia of the two transparent corneæ existed in this case.

Prof. Grasset, of Montpelier, almost at the same time as Vulpian, observed the same effects of Cocaine, but a greater persistency in the phenomena of insensibility following the intravenous injection of the solution of hydrochloride of Cocaine.

At about that time, Dr. Laborde, of the Académie de Médecine, treated still more deeply of the action of Cocaine in three successive notes to the Société de Biologie (Nov. 22d and 29th, and Dec. 27th, 1884). This learned physiologist studied the analgesic action generally resulting from subcutaneous injections of 0.03 of hydrochloride of Cocaine, in three doses, in the guinea-pig. He saw it at the same time produce a general hyper-excitability which irresistibly forced the animal to move, and even produced epileptic convulsions; the general analgesic state lasted for more than forty-eight hours.

M. Laborde, in attributing the secondary peripheric analgesia of intravenous or subcutaneous injections of hydrochlorate of Cocaine to the cerebral insusceptibility to pain, unconsciously made Cocaine a general anæsthetic.

Prof. Arloing (1885, *Mémoire Soc. Biologie*) has undertaken many experiments for demonstrating that Cocaine is not a general anæsthetic.

In his experiments, the learned physiologist of Lyons confirmed the results obtained by Vulpian as to the modifications occasioned by Cocaine of the arterial pressure ; he saw, like his predecessors, the excito-medullary and convulsary effect of large doses of Cocaine and the increase of the salivary secretion, and in regard to its cerebro-spinal effect, he compared it to strychnine. General analgesia did not occur except from fatal doses or when accompanied by convulsions. The hydrochlorate of Cocaine, according to M. Arloing, produces and can produce nothing but local anæsthesia by temporarily changing the physical properties of the protoplasm of the terminal and fibrillary nervous elements easily accessible to medicinal agents in the cornea and mucous surfaces.

We will presently show that the several learned men who have been engaged in investigating the mechanism of action of the active principles of Coca were by no means in accord as regards the *modus agendi* of Cocaine in the production of local anæsthesia.

While M. Dujardin-Beaumetz likens the local anæsthetic action of Cocaine to that of cold, and while M. Laborde considers that it produces a diminished blood supply by the vaso-constrictor action of the great sympathetic nervous system, M. Arloing, on the contrary, explains it by a local action on the nervous protoplasm.

Moreover, in 1886, Schilling, a supporter of the vascular theory, advised inhalations of nine drops of nitrite of amyl, in three doses, inhalations which caused dilatation of the vessels, to revive patients poisoned with injections of Cocaine hydrochlorate.

In repeating these experiments in the laboratory, Dr. Laffont has succeeded little by little in enlarging his field of experiments, and finally has given to the Académie de Médecine (session of the 4th of January, 1888), a complete and definitive account of the action of the active principles of Coca on the different functions of the economy. This work of original researches and criticism of previous works will serve to explain the methodical and rational use of our preparations in the list of the different diseases where our former previsions had already led us to advise them.

In an earlier work (Comptes-rendus, *Société de Biologie*, Dec. 3, 1887), Dr. Laffont, studying the action of Cocaine on the great sympathetic nervous system, found that under the action of the active principle of Coca the functions of all the constrictor fibres of the great sympathetic nerve were increased.

The stomach contracts.

The intestines undergo an augmentation in peristalsis and borborygmi are heard.

The bladder invariably contracts, as M. Laborde has also seen.

The orbital capsule of the eye (smooth muscle) propels the eye-ball forward.

The pupil is dilated.

In a word, all the smooth-fibred muscles or muscles of organic life, subordinate to the great sympathetic nervous system constrictor, undergo an augmentation of functional activity.

In a second essay (Comptes-rendus, *Société de Biologie*, Dec. 17, 1887), the same experimenter studied more particularly the mechanism of the local or general analgesic action of Cocaine, and, like M. Arloing, as opposed to M. Laborde, he found that the cerebral perceptibility was not deadened, by a physiological dose, but on the contrary, increased.

The action of Cocaine on the nervous system is not exerted by the intervention of vascular constriction; it is a generalized exciting action, and a state of peripheric non-receptivity of external impressions (1) in the nervous extremities of the sensory nerves and the nerves of general sensation.

Cocaine, according to M. Laffont, is not the antagonist of curare, as M. Laborde describes it, but quite the contrary, a particular curare, acting like it on the periphery, and not affecting the nervous centers, the functional action of which is exaggerated thereby.

M. le docteur Beugniès-Corbeau describes fully in the *Revue hebdomadaire de Thérapeutique générale et thermale*, the internal effects of Coca, until now so obscure, and in regard to which no concrete doctrine had been formulated until M. le docteur Laffont presented to the Académie de Médecine his researches. He shows that Coca, from its active principles, should have these entirely distinct actions:

1° Action on the protoplasm of the nervous extremities of the sensory nerves and on the nerves of general sensibility, producing non-transmissibility to the nerves of painful and even sensorized impressions, in a large dose;

2° Excito-functional action on the cerebro-spinal nervous centers, producing an augmentation of intellectual and muscular activity;

3° Excito-functional action on the great sympathetic constrictor nerve, consequently an exaltation of the functional action of all the non-striated muscles or muscles of organic life, which are subordinate to it.

Considering these distinct properties of the active principles of Coca, M. Laffont explains the long-recognized virtues of Coca, in that they conserve the natural forces, notwithstanding the withdrawal of aliments, in the follow-

(1) Dr. Laffont. *Etude physiologique sur la Coca et les sels de Coca.*

ing manner: " The exciting cerebro-medullary action of these principles causes an increase of the intellectual and physical activity, at the same time that the analgesic action on the extremities of the sensitive and sensory nerves, prevents the pangs of hunger, and consequently the accompanying moral and physical depression."

From another point of view, M. Laffont adds, that the dynamogenic action of the active principles of Coca on the smooth-fibered muscles "indicates its use in the list of atonic gastro-intestinal diseases, flatulent dyspepsia, dilatation of the stomach, paresis of the intestines, of the bladder, etc."

It is impossible for us to recount here all the trials which have been made with Cocaine; we will only quote the names of Dr. Deneffe, Dr. Charpentier, Dr. Morell Mackenzie, Dr. Lennox Browne, Dr. Sajous, Dr. J. Leonard Corning, Dr. Beverly Robinson, Dr. Louis Elsberg, Dr. W. Oliver Moore, Dr. Vincenzo Cozzolino, Dr. Abadie, Dr. Galezowski, Dr. Meyer, Dr. de Wecker, Dr. Doléris, Dr. David Colombe, Dr. Rigolet, and Dr. Brasseur, the majority of whom have studied this question from an ocular, therapeutical, obstetrical, dental, and laryngological point of view.

CHAPTER IV.

THERAPEUTIC ACTION OF COCA.

OW that we understand the physiological properties of Coca and Cocaine, we come to the study of the different morbid states in which these substances may be usefully employed.

DISEASES OF THE MOUTH.

Gazeau advises the use of Coca for inflammations of the mouth and gums. Pain is assuaged, ptyalism removed, and the inflammation itself favorably influenced. He cites, in support of his opinion, the use which the Peruvians make of it in affections of the mouth, and mentions cases of mercurial stomatitis treated with this agent and cured in a short time, in his practice.

Demarle (1), before him, expressed himself thus: "I have used Coca for mercurial stomatitis. The affection disappeared on the third day of treatment; nothing else had been administered."

In cases where the gums are soft, fungous, ulcerated, or bleeding, and these changes depend on local or constitutional conditions, Coca is equally indicated. Gazeau prefers it even to potassium chlorate.

(1) *Thèse de Paris*, 1862.

According to Dr. Colombe (1), Coca is a potent factor in the treatment of syphilis. (2) "It is demonstrated that potassium iodide and potassium chlorate undergo double decomposition in the system, and thus interfere with each other's action. Coca, substituted for the chlorate under such circumstances, would not be open to the same objection. It would find its application, therefore, when the mixed treatment is found necessary."

DISEASES OF THE THROAT, PHARYNX AND THE LARYNX.

As regards the *anginæ*, the acute inflammations of the larynx and pharynx, we might repeat what has been said about inflammations of the mouth. In particular, the pain, so violent in certain *anginæ*, calls for this method of treatment. The same is true of the dysphagia which accompanies them.

Charles Fauvel first recognized the virtues of Coca in the tingling of follicular *angina* and the laryngeal pains of tuberculous subjects. In those cases he specifies Mariani's extract of Coca leaves in preference to solutions of Cocaine, which sometimes give rise to symptoms of poisoning.

Dr. Rouquette (3) relates a case of tubercular laryngitis in which symptoms of poisoning showed themselves as early as the third day; the parts had been painted twice a day with a five-per-cent solution of Cocaine.

Dr. Paul Legendre has quite recently mentioned anew the danger that may result from a too free use of Co-

(1) *Thèse de Paris*, 1885.
(2) *Bumstead and Taylor on Venereal Diseases.*
(3) *Thérapeutique contemporaine*, January. 1888.

caine (1). The case was that of an interne of the hospitals attacked with diphtheria who, in order that he might the better bear the spraying with caustics, had his throat painted with a solution of Cocaine. Toward the seventh day he experienced very grave symptoms of poisoning, and the painting had to be suspended.

It is better, in cases of this sort, to prescribe extract of Coca, which answers the same purposes without the attendant danger of Cocaine.

One of the greatest triumphs of extract of Coca is assuredly its action in dysphagia and in the vomiting of consumptives, as also in the vomiting of pregnancy. The first two complications are of the gravest kind, for they condemn to starvation patients whose only chance of safety lies in the activity of the digestive organs (Ch. Fauvel and Coupard).

DISEASES OF THE STOMACH.

Authors who have given attention to Coca speak very highly of its employment in gastralgia and tardy and laborious digestion.

Demarle says on this subject : " Personally, I have found the use of Coca, either before or after eating, excellent for gastrodynia and pyrosis, to which I am subject; hardly have I swallowed the first bit of saliva when the whole unpleasant feeling disappears."

Mantegazza speaks of its use in the same strain. The cephalic congestion which accompanies his digestion is relieved; he can work after eating without feeling any uneasiness.

Dr. Ch. Gazeau (*Thèse pour le Doctorat*, Paris, 1870, Parent, édit., pp. 61 *et seq.*) thus sums up the physiological action of Coca: " On the stomach, slight excitation, anæsthesia,

(1) *Concours Médical* Aug. 11, 1888.

and probably an increase of the secretion of gastric juice ; on the intestines, an increase of the intestinal secretions, etc. These manifold physiological effects upon the digestive tube unite in a specific action, so to speak, in the numerous functional troubles, so varied and so ill-understood, of the organs that compose it."

The same author cites a great number of cases of this sort in which Coca " has never failed to exert an admirable action, often even marvelous." And he concludes (page 65) : " It seems to me useless to bring forward more examples ; these are enough to justify this positive general conclusion : Coca is the remedy *par excellence* for diseases of the digestive tube."

Beugniès-Corbeau (1) prescribes it in chloro-anæmia, not only for gastralgia, but for the frequent desire to eat which patients feel, disappearing as soon as the first mouthful has been taken, only to return a little while afterward.

Prof. O. Réveil ends his article on Coca as follows : " Much remains to be done in the physiological and clinical study of Coca ; it is known that it acts on the motor and sensory nervous system. This substance is destined some day to take an important rank in therapeutics."

In irritability and various affections of the cerebral centers, Dr. J. Leonard Corning makes use of Coca, which he prefers to the bromides.

In a very remarkable essay on *Erythroxylon Coca*, published at Ixelles, in 1885, a perusal of which we urge upon all who are interested in the study of Coca, Dr. A. Feigneau says (page 61) :

" There can be no mistake that, to a certain extent, Coca stimulates the cerebro-spinal activity by suspending or retarding the destruction of tissue in the economy, and that its action may modify the functions of the nervous centers,

(1) *Bulletin gen. de Thérap.* 1884.

provided there are no such contra-indications to its use as active congestion, inflammation, or organic changes in these organs."

"Consequently it would be indicated under all circumstances where a nervous affection seemed to depend upon a state of ataxia."

"In irritations of the spinal cord, in mental aberration accompanied by melancholia, as well as against idiopathic convulsions (Mantegazza) and nervous paraplegia."

Dr. Beverley Robinson considers the Vin Mariani as a cardiac tonic (1):

"On several occasions, when digitalis has proved to be useless or injurious, I have had very excellent results from caffeine or convallaria. Certainly, the latter drug is more easily tolerated by a sensitive stomach than digitalis is; and whenever the nervous supply of the heart is especially implicated, I believe that I secure more quieting effects from its employment. Among well known cardiac tonics and stimulants for obtaining temporary good effects, at least, I know of no drug quite equal to Coca. Given in the form of wine or fluid extract, it does much, at times, to restore the heart-muscle to its former tone. I have obtained the best effects from the use of Mariani's wine. From personal information given me by this reliable pharmacist, these results are attributable to the excellent quality of the Coca leaves and of the wine which he uses in its manufacture."

In cases of morphinomania, Dr. Dujardin-Beaumetz has pointed out the advantage to be obtained with the Vin Mariani, and, following him, Dr. Palmer, of Louisville, and Dr. Sigmaux Treux, of Vienna, have obtained excellent results with this therapeutic agent. Further on, we give a case of Dr. Villeneuve's, showing the cure of a morphinomaniac by the combined use of the Vin and the Pâte (Mariani).

(1) "Heart-strain and Weak Heart," *N. Y. Medical Record*, Feb. 26, page 238.

Dr. H. Libermann recommends the use of Coca, in the form of Vin Mariani, against morphinomania, nicotinism and alcoholism.

"In *general diseases* it is to the stimulating properties of the plant that recourse is oftenest had. These properties make it the tonic *par excellence* whenever the object is to build up a system that has been enfeebled from any cause. Its preparations, accordingly, may be ordered in convalescence from all grave fevers, in anæmia and chloro-anæmia, in all diathetic or cachætic conditions, whatever may have been their original cause (chronic rheumatism, gout, genito-urinary affection, cancer, etc.), in short, in all cases where the system is debilitated from any cause whatever."

But it is, above all, in diseases that have a depressing action on the nervous system that the effect of Coca is truly marvelous. Gubler, in his *Commentaires de thérapeutique*, shows himself its warm champion. "Coca," says he, "very much like tea and coffee, lends to the nervous system the force with which it is charged, after the manner of a fulminate, but with this difference, that it yields it gradually and not all at once."

The theory of the *fulminates*, invented by M. Gubler, tallies so well with observed facts, that Mantegazza, without generalizing and without pretending to form a theory, but limiting himself to describing by simile what he had seen, truer probably than he himself supposed, said: "Under the influence of Coca, it seems that a new force is gradually introduced into our organism, like water into a sponge." (A. Dechambre.)

This opinion has been corroborated by all authors who have given attention to the question, and it may be looked upon as one of the least contestible in therapeutics.

We will add, what is quite important, that as a tonic Coca has been found far superior to cinchona, iron, strychnine, etc. Everybody knows their astringent action, which makes them give rise to such obstinate constipation that there are patients in whom it is often necessary to suspend their use. There is no such objection to Coca; it never constipates, and practically its use may be continued indefinitely.

COCA LEAVES.

(Branch in natural state.)

CHAPTER V.

OUR VARIOUS PREPARATIONS OF COCA.

IMMEDIATELY after the importation of the Coca leaf into Europe, we conceived the plan, the outcome of the request of many physicians, of making preparations from Coca. *Vin Mariani.* —*Elixir Mariani.*—*Pâte Mariani.*—*Thé Mariani.*—*Pastilles Mariani*, etc. (The author's name was kindly added to his preparations by the medical profession, who had recognized the superiority of his products.)

These different preparations had been used by our greatest practitioners long before the discovery, or rather the application of Cocaine.

The results obtained were marvelous, and the innumerable letters which were addressed to us by physicians who experimented with and used our products and rendered accounts in the medical journals in all parts of the world, would fill several large volumes. (1)

Under the esteemed patronage of our greatest medical celebrities, our preparations are known all over the world; they have reached all classes of society and everywhere, in the large cities as in the small villages, men, women, children, in fact, convalescents of all ages now know the name of the salutary plant, which it is and has been our effort to popularize, though strictly so according to the code of medical ethics and by those channels approved of by the entire medical profession.

(1) We have on file upward of 7,000 endorsements from leading practitioners, all coinciding as to the great aid rendered by *Vin Mariani* as a tonic-stimulant.

We shall now consider the different ways in which we use Coca, and which under the well-known forms of *vin, élixir, pâte*, and of *thé Mariani*, have received such universal recognition. We will show incidentally the esteem in which these preparations are held by the highest medical authorities.

VIN MARIANI.

This is the first of the preparations of Coca and the one most generally adopted; to the tonic and stimulant action of the drug there is added that of a choice quality of wine.

Vin Mariani contains the soluble parts of the Coca plant. The combination of Coca, with the tannin and the slight traces of iron which this wine naturally contains, is pronounced the most efficacious of tonics.

The fresh Coca leaves that we employ, after careful selection, come from three different sources and are of incomparable quality. It is this that gives to our *wine* that special taste and agreeable aroma which renders it so acceptable to the sick.

It is likewise to the combination and preparing of these three varieties of Coca leaf in our wine that we can attribute this important fact; during more than thirty years, no matter in how large doses taken, *Vin Mariani* has never produced *cocainism*, nor any other unpleasant effects. (1)

Vin Mariani is a diffusible tonic, the action of which is immediate. This action, instead of being localized on a single organ, the stomach, spreads to the whole system. Taken into the circulation, it awakens in its course the retarded functions of every organ, and this is owing to the presence in our preparation of the volatile principles of the plant.

Unlike other tonics, the astringent properties of which lead at length to heat and constipation, *Vin Mariani* does

(1) It has been repeatedly proven that the many worthless, so-called Coca preparations are nothing more than variable solutions of Cocaine in inferior grades of wines or other liquids, shamefully prepared by unscrupulous or ignorant persons, whereby, in addition to the harmful effects they produce, also bring into discredit a really useful drug.

not produce any disorder of the digestive functions; it stimulates them, exerts a refreshing action on the gastric mucous membrane, and on that account so advantageously replaces the preparations of cinchona, iron, strychnine, etc.

"There is," says Dr. Mallez, "a form of anæmia to which the attention of physicians has not yet been called, and which yields marvelously to the employment of *Vin Mariani;* we allude to that state of profound depression of the economy, of extremely marked impoverishment of the blood, which also results from the prolonged abuse of balsamics in the treatment of diseases of the urinary passages.

"The number of persons who, attacked with blennorrhagia, use cubebs, copaiba, turpentine, etc., to a deplorable extent is considerable. So true is this that, out of a hundred young dyspeptics, we may affirm without fear of being in error that at least forty of them have become so by the use of balsamics.

"In like manner, the number of patients affected with urinary gravel whom the prolonged and excessive use of the agents just mentioned, has rendered dyspeptic and then neuropathic is enormous. Like the former, they owe the profound disorder of their digestive functions to the immoderate use of resins and oleo-resins.

"It is of the first importance, therefore, to relieve these persons by making them take, after having given them light laxatives and some preparations intended to strengthen the stomach, not iron, not cinchona, not, as we have said above, local tonics, which would be of little if any use, but diffusible tonics, that is to say, those that act upon the local condition and at the same time upon the general condition, and which, moreover, do not constipate.

"It is here that *Vin Mariani* proves its great advantage and succeeds where other tonics have failed, in stimulating the functions of the stomach. On the one hand by the small quantity of tannin which it contains, on the other through the active principles of Coca, associated with the wine, which serves as a vehicle, exciting the vitality of each organ separately, not, however, without having previously exerted its vivifying action on the mucous membrane of the stomach itself." (*Gazette des Hopitaux*, Nov. 23, 1877.)

The analgesic properties of *Vin Mariani* have received a happy application in clinical laryngoscopy by Dr. Ch. Fauvel. This eminent specialist has made use of it for the past twenty-six years with unvarying success in all affections of the laryngeal mucous membrane, the air passages, and the vocal organs. In granular angina it takes the place of the topical medication and cauterizations which are so often injurious when they are used indiscriminately and to excess.

The employment of *Vin Mariani* rapidly relieves patients of the feeling of heat and tingling which is one of the most annoying symptoms of this very common disease of the throat. (*Gazette des Hopitaux*, May 12, 1877.)

Dr. Beverley Robinson recommends *Vin Mariani* as a heart tonic.

Dr. W. H. Pancoast says that *Vin Mariani* is a valuable preparation and a tonic of the highest merit.

Dr. Jules Bouvyer, of Cauteretz, employs it with success in certain affections of the larynx as an adjuvant to the sulphurous treatment.

In 1875, in his *Traitement rationnel de la phthisie pulmonaire* Dr. de Pietra Santa said, page 394 :

"Among the most renowned practitioners of Paris, Péan, Barth, G. Sée, and Cabrol have promptly adopted the preparations of Coca. Ch. Fauvel prescribes it in affections of the respiratory passages. It is in these diseases that I, too, have had occasion to advise its daily use in the most convenient, the most agreeable, and the most active form—that of the *Vin Tonique de Mariani.*"

Thus has been realized Réveil's prediction : "This substance (Coca) is destined to take an important rank in therapeutics."

In the *Revue de Thérapeutique médicaux-chirurgicale*, June 11, 1876, page 381. Bibliographie: *Dictionnaire Encyclopédique des sciences médicales*, par A. Dechambre, Dr. H. Cottin thus closes his article:

" In France, we are using a great deal of Coca wine, and it is tending to take the place of all other tonic wines; it is borne a longer time by the stomach and is more agreeable to the palate. M. Mariani has contributed much to the popularization of Coca by the perfection of his preparations, *vin, thé élixir* and *pâte*. These are the forms at present most employed."

Dr. Chapusot, of Paris, thus sums up his personal observations: "A claret-glass of this wine has always been enough to make me forget hunger and to sustain my strength; I have felt a grateful warmth and a general exaltation of the economy; the digestion of the following meal has always been easier than if I had not taken the *Vin Mariani*, and, although I had not such a ravenous appetite as if I had gone without it, I ate a good deal, the stomach appearing stronger and more active."

It was Dr. Ch. Fauvel who gave our wine the very striking and exact title of "Tensor of the vocal cords." He says: "Thanks to *Vin Mariani*, I have been able to restore the voice of many lyric artists who would have been unable without this potent agent to give their performances."

Dr. J. Leonard Corning, in *Brain Exhaustion*, New York, 1884, pages 78 and 112, says: "Of all the medicaments that I employ in the very numerous cases of irritability, *Vin Mariani* has rendered the greatest service. I do not except even the bromides, for this preparation of Coca possesses the calmative properties of those salts without producing the unpleasant depression which characterizes them."

The same author continues:

"The *Vin Mariani* is the remedy *par excellence* for *ennui*.

At the same time it produces a fortifying action on the cerebral center and gives rise to a decided sensation of well-being."

Dr. Morell Mackenzie, London, advises the *Vin Mariani* as a stimulant and tonic, and uses it especially with speakers and singers.

19 Harley Street,
Cavendish Square, W., London.

Gentlemen:—I have much pleasure in stating that I have used the *Vin Mariani* for many years, and consider it a valuable stimulant, particularly serviceable in the cases of vocalists.

Yours faithfully,

Morell Mackenzie, M. D.

Professor Sajous, of Philadelphia, who has experimented with *Vin Mariani* in troubles of the vocal organs, has obtained excellent results from its use, and he advises it, not only as a restorative of the voice, but as a general tonic.

Dr. Libermann, Surgeon-in-Chief, French Army, communicates his experience, as follows:

"I have the honor to inform you of the results which I have obtained in my long career of military practice from the use of *Vin Mariani*.

"I have used it with great success for profound anæmia resulting from long and tedious campaigns in hot countries, and accompanied, as is nearly always the case, by gastro-intestinal irritation with loss of appetite and dyspepsia. Two or three Bordeaux-glasses of *Vin Mariani* daily, removed that condition quite rapidly, by restoring the appetite and the tolerance of the stomach for a tonic aliment.

"I have also employed it in cases, happily rare in our army, of chronic alcoholism resulting from the abuse of brandy, absinthe or strong liquors. The *Vin Mariani* produced all the excitement sought by drinkers, but had at the same time a sedative influence on their nervous systems. I have frequently seen hardened drinkers renounce their fatal habit and return to a healthy condition.

"I have also used *Vin Mariani* to save smokers of exaggerated habits, from nicotinism. A few glasses of *Vin Mariani* taken in small doses, either pure or mixed with water, acted as a substitute for pipes and cigars, because the smokers found in it the cerebral excitement which they sought in tobacco, wholly preserving their intellectual faculties.

"I have also employed it with success for chronic bronchitis and pulmonary phthisis. *Vin Mariani* increases the appetite and diminishes the cough in these two morbid states.

"To combat the cough I give it mixed with water in the form of tisane, a Bordeaux-glass of *Mariani* in a glass of hot water.

"Besides I have used it to the greatest advantage in convalescence from typhoid fever, when no wine, not even Bordeaux, was retained by the stomach on account of gastric irritation which is the rule after fevers of this nature.

"Although I have confined myself to giving but a rapid glance at the results that I have obtained, I have the statistics, which I keep in reserve should they be needed.

"I can certify that *Vin Mariani* is the most powerful weapon that can be put in the hands of military physicians to combat the diseases, the infirmities, and even the vicious habits engendered by camp life and the servitude of military existence."

Dr. Villeneuve, among other cases of morphinomania conquered by the combined use of the *pâte* and the *Vin Mariani*, communicated to us in 1884 the following observation:

"M. X ....., barrister, 32 years of age, five years ago began to use morphine preparations as a remedy against a very alarming chronic bronchitis and granulations in the throat, which were irritated constantly by cigarette smoking.

"The patient at first only used morphine, but his physicians committed the imprudence of treating him by hypodermic injection. A notable change for the better was produced during the first month, but, unfortunately, abuse succeeded promptly the use of the medicament— so much so that when I commenced to treat the patient, he was taking daily from 1 gramme 50 centigrammes to 1 gramme 80 centigrammes of morphine hypodermically. When he was four hours without his dose there appeared insomnia, hallucinations and delirium; constipation lasting sometimes for fifteen days, which brought on in the spring a very alarming perityphlitis, jerking of the muscles, sudden frights, dyspepsia, and at last frightful congestion of the face whenever he drank a drop of wine or brandy.

"After a month's treatment I had succeeded in reducing the daily doses without causing alarming symptoms; the physiological functions seemed to awaken again. However, the congestion and especially the dyspepsia was very grave, and the cough which had been suppressed by morphine returned. It was then that I treated my patient with phosphate of lime, the *pâte* and the *Vin Mariani*. Lacking his habitual stimulant, he was plunged in a semi-coma from which he could not always be relieved with weaker daily doses of morphine.

"The danger I feared most was a relapse of bronchitis, and that the cough and expectoration might end fatally. But in about a week, during which he took ten doses of *Pâte de Coca* daily, the cough became less fatiguing and disappeared entirely in about twenty days. The patient then commenced to take small doses of *Vin Mariani* (two Madeira-glasses a day). At first congestion appeared, but little by little, as digestion became more easy, my patient, who on account of his profound anæmia could not tolerate any table wines, took at first a small glass, then two, then three glasses at a meal. Now he can go and take his dinner in town, which he had not been able to do for three years; he regained his former vigor, is able to undertake anew his occupations, and has entirely given up his morphine habit."

We will conclude our quotations, already too numerous, with an article by Dr. Scaglia, published in 1877 in the *Gazette des Hopitaux:* "La Coca et ses propriétés thérapeutiques."

"In anæmia, connected with chronic pulmonary affections without fever, and in anæmia accompanied by gastralgia, *Vin Mariani* has an excellent effect. Its stimulating properties can also be admirably made use of in those intermediate states of impaired health which are not yet anæmia, but must in the end become so; physical or mental overwork, the cerebral weakness due to excess of work or pleasure; the exhaustion from which the inhabitants of large cities suffer through irregularities of diet and imperfect hygiene owing to their positions and surroundings.

"*Vin Mariani* is unquestionably of benefit to people of sedentary habits worn out by work, to convalescents who, from a prolonged confinement in bed, have lost muscular strength, to patients suffering from diabetes or Bright's disease, whose muscles have lost their elasticity and vigor.

"Let us add that the taste of *Vin Mariani* is exquisite, that it is in no way suggestive of drugs, and that its use is acceptable to the most fastidious."

Ordinary Dose—Two or three claret-glassfuls daily, half an hour before or immediately after eating.

COCA GROG.—By mixing a wineglassful of *Vin Mariani* with half a glassful of boiling water, sweetened to the taste, we get a grog of exquisite flavor, and capable of rendering the greatest services whenever an immediate effect is desired in severe cases of cold, attended by convulsive coughing. (As prescribed by Dr. Libermann, Dr. Cyrus Edson and others, recorded in the medical journals during the grip epidemics.)

ELIXIR MARIANI.

The *Elixir Mariani* is more alcoholic, very agreeable to the taste, and three times as highly charged with the aromatic principles of the Coca leaf as the *Vin Mariani*; therefore it should be taken in doses of a liqueur-glassful, in the morning upon rising, and after the two principal meals.

It may be used clear or mixed with water, in nearly all cases where the *Vin Mariani* is used. Its tonic and eminently digestive properties and its special aroma, at once mild and penetrating, make it an agreeable liqueur, very much esteemed by gourmets and persons who are careful about their health.

A small glass of the *Elixir Mariani* taken after a meal, spreads a gentle warmth through the stomach and calls forth an abundant secretion of gastric juice, which mixes with the food and facilitates digestion.

For travelers, hunters, and in general all who walk much and who are exposed to fatigue, to dampness, and to fog, the use of the *Elixir Mariani* may be recommended and will render admirable service, because of the tone and strength that it gives to the stomach and to the muscles.

Dr. Collins, *Révue de Thérapeutique*, observes that this liqueur acts "heroically" in anæmia, chlorosis and rickets.

Dr. Ch. Fauvel, Dr. Conqueret, Dr. Villeneuve, Dr. Chapusot, Dr. Odin, Dr. Cintrat and others declare as the result of their clinical observations that the *Elixir Mariani* exerts a "masterly action" in granular pharyngitis, quinsy, and albuminuria, and that its stimulating properties on the whole nervous system cannot be denied.

Dr. J. Leonard Corning, of New York, recommends the *Elixir Mariani* as a strengthener of the brain.

"As a remedy in *sea-sickness*, the *Elixir Mariani* has

always given excellent results."—Dr. Blant, Dr. Letellier, Dr. Trossat, Dr. Derrecagaix.

The *Elixir Mariani* is generally prescribed in doses of a liqueur-glassful after the principal meals. Mixed with cold water, in the proportion of two liqueur-glassfuls to a tumbler of water, it constitutes a very strengthening and pleasant drink.

PÂTE MARIANI (LOZENGES OF COCA).

Tonic and pectoral, *Pâte Mariani* is a Lozenge very agreeable to the taste, which is prescribed daily with the greatest success by throat specialists for obstinate coughs, granular catarrh of the throat, and the various inflammations of the digestive and respiratory passages. Composed only of clarified gum, sugar and Coca, without a trace of opium or of any narcotic substances, it may be taken without danger at any hour of the day and in any quantity, without fear of its disturbing the digestion, since, on the contrary, it can only aid it. From six to ten of the Lozenges daily are the usual dose, but more may be taken if necessary.

Its beneficial action is due to the happy combination of the emolient properties of pure gum-arabic and the tonic, astringent and analgesic properties of Coca.

"*Pâte Mariani* has a powerful tonic action on the larynx, and, like *Vin Mariani*, it is invaluable in cases of aphonia caused by feebleness or relaxation of the vocal cords. This property is of special advantage to singers and orators. *Pâte Mariani* is a very valuable substitute in granular catarrh of the throat and throat affections in general, for chlorate of potassium pastilles and the various lozenges containing opium, etc., the *Pâte Mariani* is more agreeable to the taste and produces anæsthetic and soothing effects." (*Gazette des Hopitaux.*)

PASTILLES MARIANI (COCA AND COCAINE).

The *Pastilles Mariani* are used in the same cases as the *Pâte*, from which they differ only by the addition of two milligrammes of Cocaine hydrochlorate to each pastille.

Their action is much more intense and more rapid than that of the plain Coca Lozenges.

The paroxysms of cough which are so frequent and so annoying to those who smoke tobacco to excess, are overcome as if by enchantment by the use of a few pastilles.

Dose—Four to eight daily. This amount, however, may be exceeded, at the discretion of the physicians.

THÉ MARIANI, OR CONCENTRATED EXTRACT OF COCA (TEA MARIANI).

As its name indicates, Mariani's concentrated extract of Coca, or *Thé Mariani*, contains within a small bulk all the active principles of the Coca leaf. This extract, prepared in special apparatuses which prevent all alteration and preserve all its properties and all its aroma, answers entirely in the various modes of using Coca and constitutes a most scrupulously exact preparation in dose, the most convenient and the most active that could be desired.

Thé Mariani is capable of indefinite preservation and easy of transportation; it renders great service to persons who make mountain ascensions, fatiguing marches, or long journeys through unhealthy countries, and in fact in whatever may be called fatiguing work or pleasure.

Thé Mariani may be taken in the dose of from three to six teaspoonfuls in the course of the day, clear, or mixed with brandy, wine, water or milk, etc., hot or cold, in the latter cases sweetened to taste, if desired.

COCA TEA OR INFUSION.—A teaspoonful of the *Thé Mariani*, added to a cup of hot water, sweetened to the taste, with or without the addition of cream or milk, makes a very agreeable drink, more digestive, more tonic, and less exciting than coffee or tea, while possessing in a higher degree the tonic and stimulating properties of those two substances.

It is in this form that Coca is especially used in Peru and Bolivia, where it is preferred to the Chinese tea.

Persons who drink Chinese tea at meals may advantageously substitute the *Thé Mariani* for it.

For patients who cannot generally take milk, it is advisable to add *Thé Mariani*. Excellent results will be obtained.

COCA GARGLES AND SPRAYS.—Independently of its tonic and reconstituent action, Coca possesses anæsthetic and soothing properties that have been observed and made use of in practice by laryngologists in the form of a spray, in the proportion of a teaspoonful of *Thé Mariani* to half a glassful of warm water.

An ambulance physician of Tonkin, who has experimented with *Thé Mariani*, sends the following note:

"*Thé Mariani* has rendered us real service during expeditions as well as in hospital practice; on the march it makes with boiled water, with or without the addition of sugar, a very agreeable, tonic and stimulating drink; a veritable reserve food, it takes the place of alcoholic drinks and insufficiency of food, and aids the men in bearing the most distressing fatigue. The water of swamps, rivers or ditches, mixed with a few spoonfuls of *Thé Mariani*, could be drank without any inconvenience, and assuaged thirst.

"*Thé Mariani* stimulates the appetite, overcomes atony of the digestive organs, and prevents and combats diarrhœa efficiently.

"Mixed in small quantity with fresh or condensed milk, it gives it an agreeable taste and causes it to be borne by the most delicate stomachs; hence it becomes a valuable adjuvant in the treatment of the endemic dysenteries and diarrhœas of tropical countries.

"Finally, its exclusive use, even its excessive use for several days, has not seemed to us to exert any injurious influence on the system, as the abuse of coffee or of alcoholic drinks had certainly done under like circumstances."

Dr. Fordyce Barker, Dr. J. H. Douglas, Dr. Henry B. Sands and Dr. Geo. F. Shrady have authorized us to make known that it was due to *Thé Mariani*, added to milk (in the proportion of a teaspoonful of the *Thé* to a cup of milk), that they were able to nourish Gen. Grant, the ex-President, when he was unable to support any other food. By this means they succeeded in prolonging the life of their illustrious patient for several months.

Coca taken in infusion gave excellent results to Tschudy while he was sojourning in the valley of the Puna, the highest in Bolivia, which has given its name to the disease of mountain sickness, known in Peru by the name *Mal de Puna*, also designated by the words *sorroche, veta* and *marco;* this last term shows clearly enough the analogy which exists between sea-sickness and the influence of great altitudes on the human body. Experience has proved the usefulness of Coca against dyspnœa and vomiting, so that the Indians who make ascensions always carry a stock of Coca with them. Dr. Tschudy found himself comfortable by the use of it while hunting in those valleys, at a height of ten to twelve thousand feet above the sea.

Dr. Salemi, of Nice, gives an account of a case of epilepsy in a woman, 38 years of age, cured by the daily and prolonged use of *Thé Mariani*, given in increasing doses (ten drops daily at first and eighty drops daily at the end of a month). This case is not an isolated one.

IMPORTANT CAUTION.

Owing to the success obtained by our preparations of Coca for many years, imitators and counterfeiters have dared to apply to their own valueless productions the observations made with our special products. These occurrences, often repeated, have given rise to protests from many physicians, among others Dr. W. Oliver Moore, Sir Morell Mackenzie, Dr. Ch. Fauvel.

To the Editor of the New York Medical Journal:

SIR: In your issue of January 3, 1885, page 19, in a report of a paper read before the New York Medical Society, on "The Physiological and Therapeutical Effects of the Coca Leaf and its Alkaloid," occurs the following: "For over twenty years Dr. Fauvel has used it, both internally in the form of *Vin Mariani*, and also by local applications to the pharynx and larynx in spray or by brush, in the form of a fluid extract, or, more recently, of a concentrated non-alcoholic preparation more of the nature of a cordial (prepared by Mariani & Co.)."

Several manufacturers of Coca preparations have taken occasion to quote from this paper, each in turn substituting the name of *his own* production instead of the one mentioned in the original.

As the preparations of Coca mentioned in my paper were personally tested and found to be the best of a large number experimented with, I wish to call attention to these misquotations and substitutions.

Very truly,

W. OLIVER MOORE, M.D.

*** We have taken the trouble to compare the report of Dr. Moore's remarks with the little book on Coca prepared by M. Mariani, and with the circulars issued by a number of manufacturers of Coca preparations; and we certainly think that some of these manufacturers have taken an unwarrantable liberty in appropriating work that evidently cost M. Mariani a good deal of time and no little outlay of money.—EDITOR *N. Y. Medical Journal.*

New York Medical Journal. October 24, 1885.

"In another column we publish a letter from Dr. W. Oliver Moore, calling attention to an injustice that certain competing pharmacists have practiced toward Messrs. Mariani & Co., in 'pirating' published records of the successful use of the Mariani preparations of Coca, and at the same time craftily making these records appear to apply to their own preparations. It is very much to be regretted that a house that has been so punctilious in avoiding even the semblance of any offense against the courtesy of trade should have been treated in this shabby way by some rival manufacturers."

---

31 RUE GUÉNÉGAUD, PARIS, Dec. 8, 1887.
To the Editor of the New York Medical Journal:

SIR—Will you kindly have it announced in your journal, in justice to myself before the medical profession, that the various notices appearing in journals and circulars quoting my name in connection with Coca are entirely false and in every respect a prevarication? The only preparation of Coca employed by me with undoubted and uniform success has been the so well-known *Vin Mariani*, which, since 1865, I have had occasion to prescribe daily in my *clinique*, as well as in private practice. My opinion of this valuable medicament has, during many years, been frequently made known for the benefit of the profession in various writings, and it is but just to this worthy preparation that it receive all the honor due it. I thank you for compliance with my request.

CH. FAUVEL, M.D.

Continued compliment is paid M. Mariani for the maintained high standard and excellence of his preparations, by the numerous honorable mentions and indorsements by the members of the medical profession and those who have occasion to use his Coca preparations; latterly through the following awards:

Gold Medal and Silver Medal from the Académie Nationale de France; Gold Medal and a Grand Diploma of Honor from the Wine Exhibit of Bordeaux, France; Gold Medal and a Diploma of Honor at the Hygienic Exhibit at Amsterdam, Holland, and a Gold Medal and Diploma at Leamington, England, the jury surnaming his *Vin Mariani*, "Wine for Athletes."

N. B.—Professional bicyclists and athletes, after careful trials of ours and preparations of others, among which the Cafeine, Theobromine, Kola, pseudo-Cafeine or Kolamine (Knebel), Maté, etc., invariably give the preference to our Coca preparation. Messrs. Dubois, Lucas, Vigneaux, Echalié, André Henry, Imans, Buffel, and many others have attested to the vast superiority of Coca Mariani over all other tonics (dynamogéniques).

We request those physicians, who kindly place confidence in our preparations, to prescribe them under the name of *Mariani*, and to insist that their prescriptions be scrupulously executed.

PLATE I.

TRANSVERSE SECTION OF A YOUNG BRANCH; PRIMARY FORMATIONS.

(See Plate III., Figure 3.)

Ec., Bark formed of an epidermis *Ep.*, of a parenchyma (pulp) well developed with some oxaliferous cellules *C. o.* On the section is seen a bundle of libero-ligneous stipulaires *F. s.*

F. p., Fibres péricycliques.

Li., Liber, with oxaliferous cellules *C. o.*

B., Wood.

Mo., Pulpy pith containing cellules of ligneous dotted partitions *C.l.*, and oxaliferous cellules. The cortical and medullary pulp contain in their cellules numberless grains of starch, which are not indicated in this plate.

PLATE I.

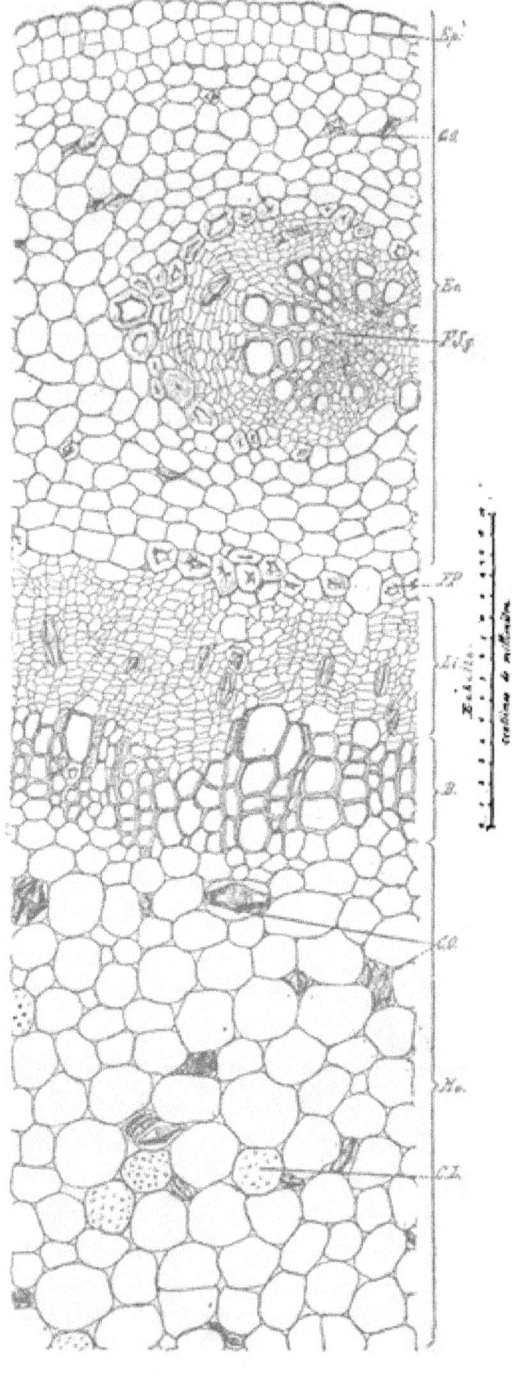

PLATE II.

Fig. 1—TRANSVERSE SECTION OF AN AGED STEM; SECONDARY FORMATIONS.

Fig. 2—LONGITUDINAL SECTION OF SAME STEM.

Bark formed of a corky and pulpy cortical of a secondary origin. The primary bark exfoliates itself at a very early stage.

The pulp contains some oxaliferous cellules and some grains of starch.

The wood contains some veins and a considerable quantity of fibres with thick and dotted partitions. The marrow remains always pulpy and with lignified cellules.

PLATE II.

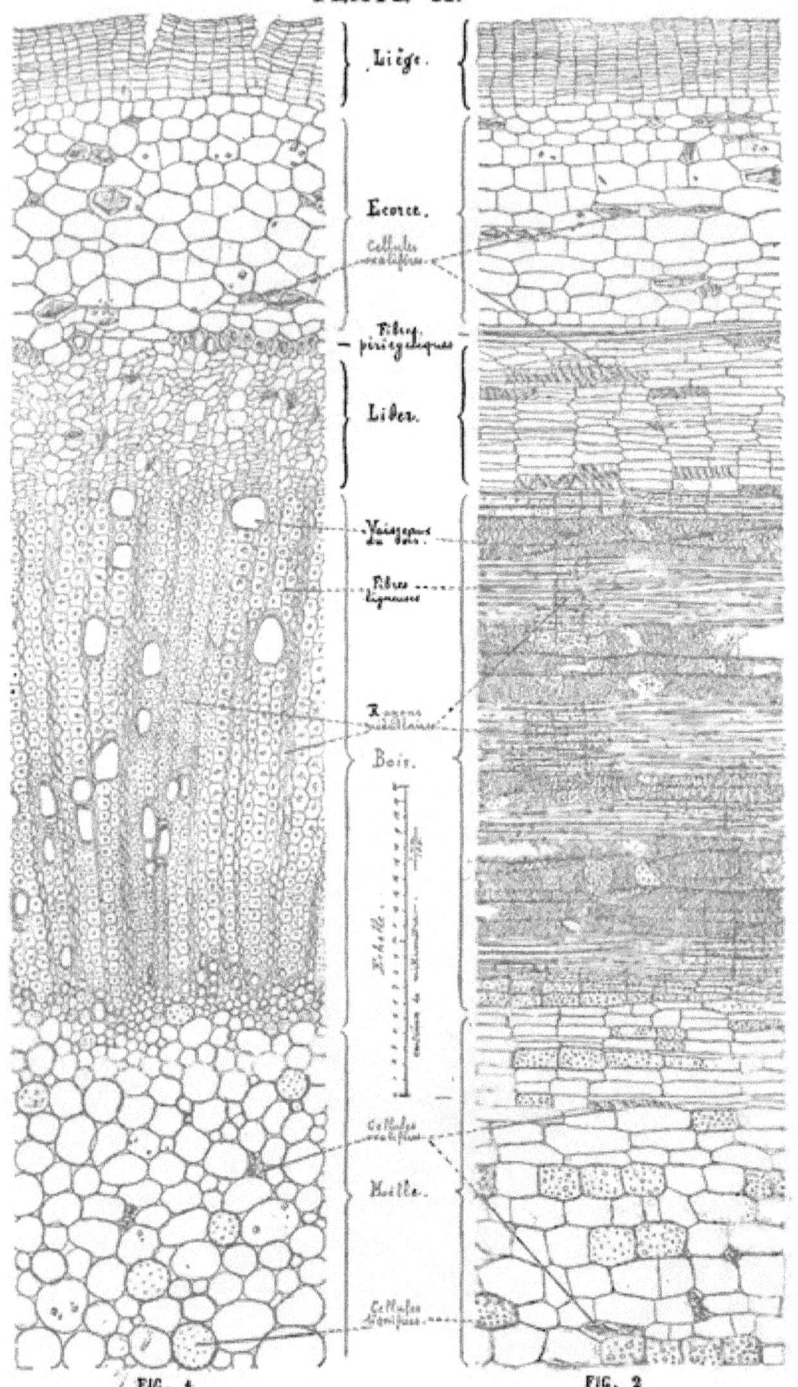

FIG. 1.   FIG. 2.

PLATE III.

Fig. 1—TRANSVERSE SECTION OF A PRIMARY ROOT.

$A. p.$, Heaped layer.
$A. s.$, Corky layer.
$Ec.$, Pithy bark.
$End.$, Endoderm ; the thickening of the lateral partitions of its cellules is very apparent.
$P.$, Pericycle formed of a single layer of cellules.
$T. c.$, Conjunctive tissue or pith.
$B.$, Ligneous fasciculous ; there are two to the diameter.
$L.$, Liberian fasciculous ; there are two to the diameter, perpendicular to the preceding.

Fig. 2—TRANSVERSE SECTION OF A ROOT ; SECONDARY FORMATIONS.

$L. s.$, Cork, secondary.
$Ec. s.$, Bark, secondary ; the primary formations are exfoliate.
$L.$, Liber.
$F. l.$, Ligneous fibres in large numbers and meatus.
$V.$, Veins of wood, dotted.
$R. m.$, Medullary radius.
$M. s.$, Pith which has become entirely sclerotic.

Fig. 3—SCHEMATIC SECTION OF A YOUNG BRANCH.

$Ec.$, Bark.
$F. f.$, Foliated fasciculous not yet separated from the central cylinder.
$F. s.$, Fasciculous stipulaire.
$Mo.$, Pith.
$Z. g.$, Generating zone libero-ligneous.

Fig. 4—GRAINS OF STARCH OF THE SEED.

(Maximum dimensions : 22 to 24 p. x 15 to 16 p.)

PLATE III.

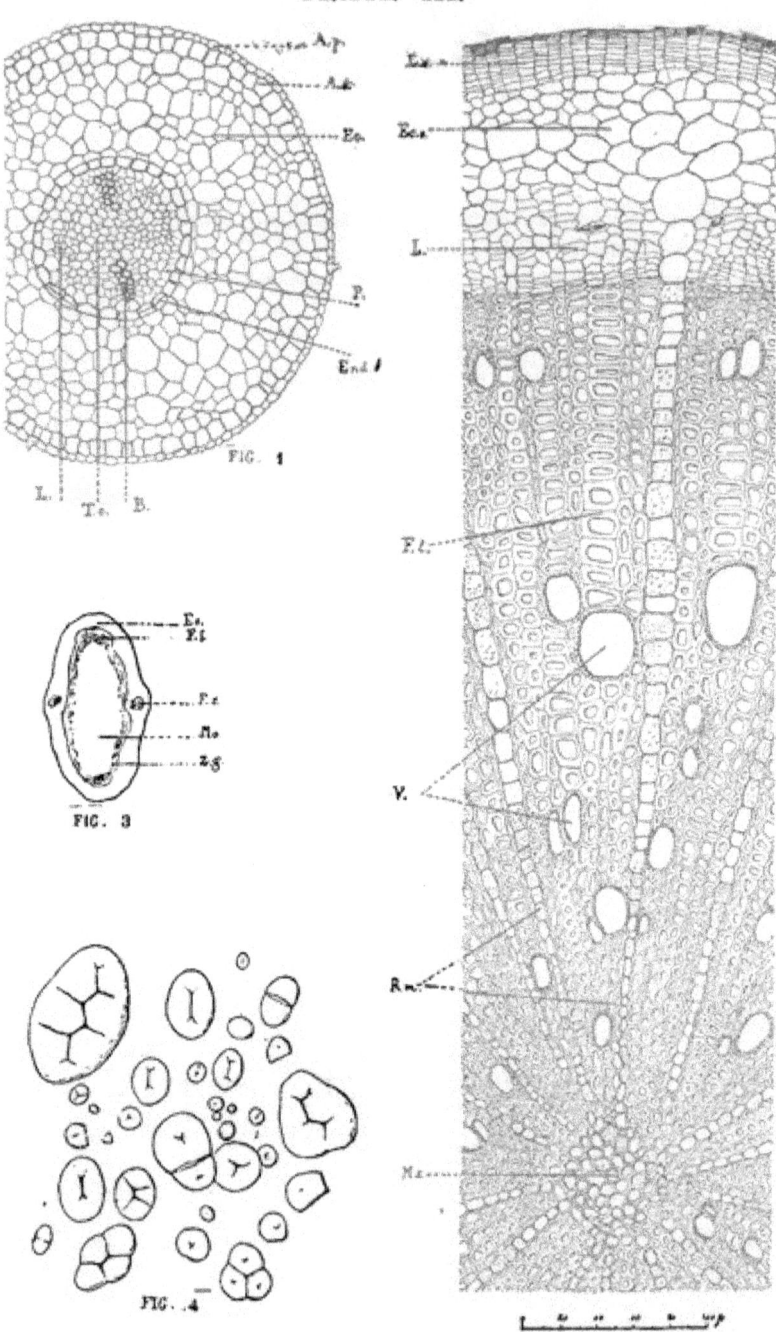

PLATE IV.

Fig. 1—FOLIATION. TRANSVERSE SECTION OF A LEAF NOT YET UNROLLED, SHOWING THE TWO LONGITUDINAL JUTTINGS WHICH FORM THE FALSE NERVURES OF THE COCA LEAF.

$F. i.$, Lower surface.
$F. S.$, Upper surface.
$N. p.$, Principal nervure.
$F. n.$, False nervures.

Fig. 2—TRANSVERSE SECTION OF ONE OF THE JUTTINGS.

$E. s.$, Upper epidermis.
$E. i.$, Lower epidermis.
$F. n.$, False nervure.

Fig. 3—LOWER EPIDERMIS OF THE LEAF AT THE FALSE NERVURE $F. n.$, WHICH IS FORMED OF LENGTHENED CELLULES WITHOUT STOMATUM $S.$, STOMATUM $P.$, EPIDERMIC PAPILLOUS CELLULES.

Fig. 4—TRANSVERSE SECTION OF A LEAF ENTIRELY DEVELOPED.

$E. s.$, Upper epidermis.
$E. i.$, Lower epidermis.
$P.$, Parenchyme foliate.
$C. p.$, Palissadique cellules.
$C. s.$, Sclerotic cellules.
$L. a.$, Air-conveying cell.
$F. l. l.$, Fasciculous libero ligneous.

Fig. 5—SCHEMATIC SECTION OF A PETIOL NEAR THE BASE.

Fig. 6—EXTREMITY OF A BRANCH SHOWING THE STIPULES OF THE LEAVES.

Fig. 7—TWO STIPULES CONNECTED, SEEN FROM THE BRANCHED SURFACE.

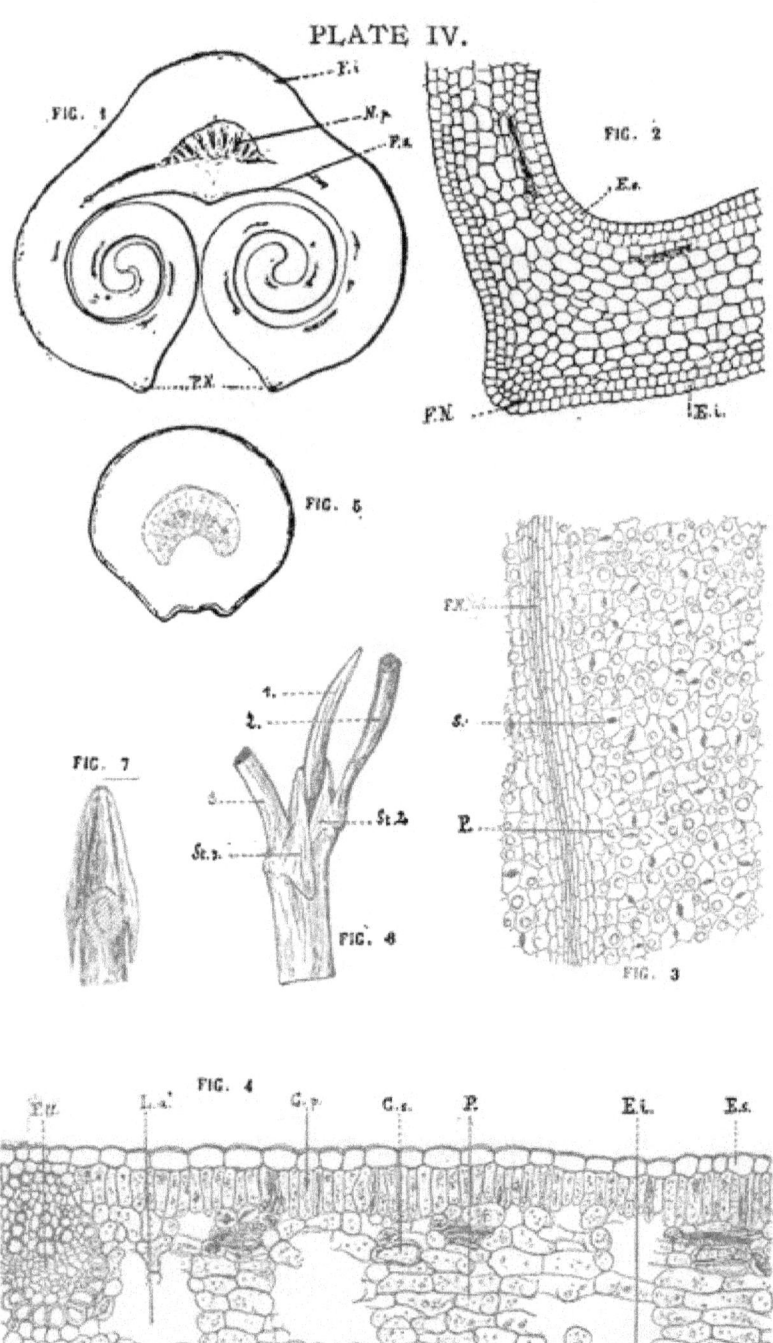

PLATE V.

Fig. 1—RIPE SEED; THE THREE STYLES AND THE STAMENS ARE STILL ADHERENT.

Fig. 2—LONGITUDINAL SECTION OF SAME.

    $T. g.$, Tegument of the seed.
    $A.$, Amylaceous albumen.
    $R.$, Embryo rootlet.
    $C.$, Cotyledons.

Fig. 3—SCHEMATIC SECTION OF THE HALF-DEVELOPED SEED.

    $P. c.$, Carpellary pulp.
    $C. a.$, Abortive carpelle.
    $T. o.$, Tegument ovarium.
    $A. a.$, Amylaceous albumen.
    $C. e.$, Embryo cotyledons.
    $N. t.$, Nervure of tegument of the ovule.

Fig. 4—TRANSVERSE SCHEMATIC SECTION OF A COTYLEDON.

Fig. 5—FLORAL BUD.

Fig. 6—AN EXPANDED FLOWER.

Fig. 7—THE SAME, SEEN FROM UNDERNEATH.

Fig. 8—TWO PETALS, ONE SEEN FROM UNDERNEATH, THE OTHER SEEN SIDEWAYS AND SHOWING THE APPENDIX WHICH FORMS THE CROWN.

Fig. 9—THE ATTACHED 10 STAMENS; THE EPIPETALS ARE LARGER THAN THE EPISEPALS.

Fig. 10—AN ANTHER AND THREAD OF STAMEN.

Fig. 11—POLLEN SEEDS.
(Dimensions: 35 p. x 28 p.)

Fig. 12—STYLE AND STIGMATE.

Fig. 13—FLORAL DIAGRAM.
The floral formula is: $[5\ S] + 5\ P + [10\ E] - [3\ C]$.

PLATE V.

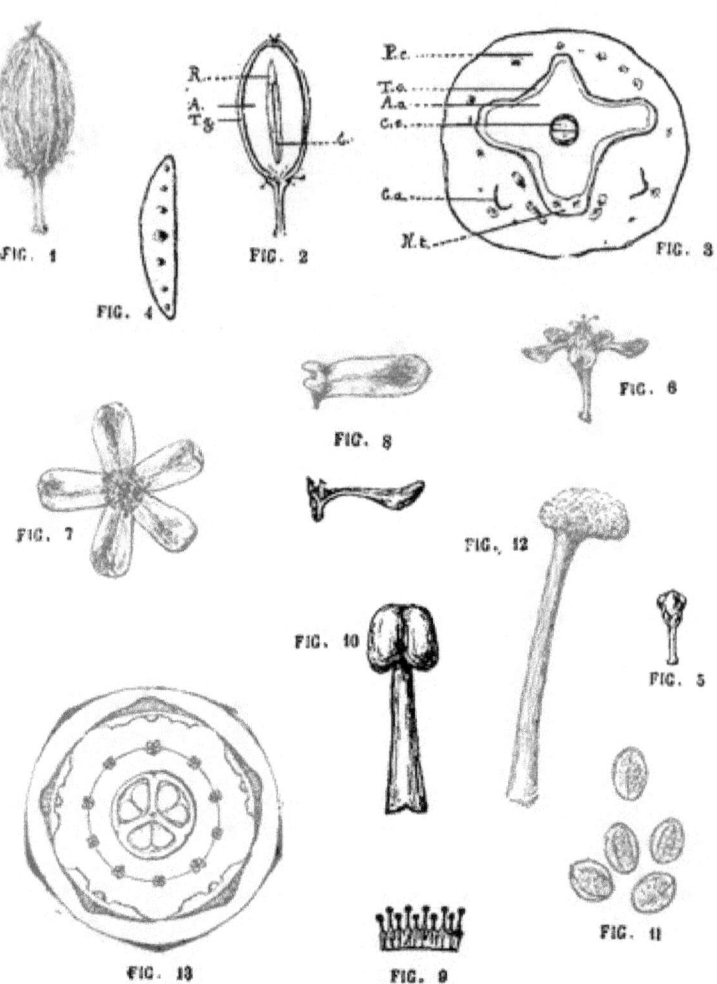

"Mariani Bottle" showing Shape and Label.

We are justified in saying:
Never has anything been so highly recommended and every trial proves its excellence.

"Mariani Bottle" showing Outside Wrapper.

Size of Regular Bottle, half litre (about 17 ounces).

Never sold in bulk—to guard against substitution.

VIN MARIANI

Nourishes - Fortifies
Refreshes
Aids Digestion - Strengthens the System.

Unequaled as a tonic-stimulant for fatigued or overworked Body and Brain.

Prevents Malaria, Influenza and Wasting Diseases.

We cannot aim to gain support for our preparation through cheapness; we give a uniform, effective and honest article, and respectfully ask personal testing of **Vin Mariani** strictly on its own merits. Thus the medical profession can judge whether **Vin Mariani** is deserving of the unequaled reputation it has earned throughout the world during more than 30 years.

Inferior, so-called Coca preparations (variable solutions of Cocaine and cheap wines), which have been proven worthless, even harmful in effect, bring into discredit and destroy confidence in a valuable drug.

We therefore particularly caution to specify always " VIN MARIANI," thus we can guarantee invariable satisfaction to physician and patient.

www.ingramcontent.com/pod-product-compliance
Lightning Source LLC
Chambersburg PA
CBHW020333090426
42735CB00009B/1527